FOOD, WINE & FRIENDS

FOOD, WINE & FRIENDS

simple menus for great entertaining

FIONA BECKETT

photography by Peter Cassidy

RYLAND
PETERS
& SMALL

LONDON NEW YORK

Dedication
For Will and Maria

First published in the United Kingdom
in 2007
by Ryland Peters & Small
20–21 Jockey's Fields
London WC1R 4BW
www.rylandpeters.com

10 9 8 7 6 5 4 3 2 1

ISBN: 978 1 84597 464 0

A catalogue record for this book
is available from the British Library.

Printed and bound in China.

Design and Photographic Art Direction
  Steve Painter
Editor Julia Charles
Production Gemma Moules
Publishing Director Alison Starling

Food Stylist Annie Rigg
Prop Stylist Helen Trent
Indexer Hilary Bird

Notes

• All spoon measurements are level, unless
otherwise stated.

• Eggs are medium unless otherwise specified.
Please note that the recipes on pages 25, 42, 95
and 119 contain raw eggs. Uncooked or partially
cooked eggs should not be served to the very old,
frail, young children, pregnant women or those
with compromised immune systems.

• Ovens should be preheated to the specified
temperature. Recipes in this book were tested
using a regular oven. If using a fan-assisted oven,
follow the manufacturer's instructions for
adjusting temperatures.

• All herbs used in these recipes are fresh unless
otherwise specified.

contents

the menus

how wine can enhance your enjoyment of food

Food, wine and friends. Can there be a better formula for an evening's entertainment? No one element is as good in isolation. Friends without food or wine: good to see them, but it can all seem rather rushed. Food without wine or friends: functional rather than fun. Wine without food or friends simply isn't as enjoyable at all.

Countries where wine is a part of life, like France and Italy, know this instinctively. The wine goes on the table automatically – they know the food tastes better as a result. It helps relax your guests and aids digestion, helping you to savour each mouthful more intensely. Sipping wine slows down the pace of the meal.

It also – and this hasn't yet fully been recognized – helps the busy host or hostess make an impact with their entertaining. If you've bought a ready-made or takeaway meal (as so many of us do these days), your guests will more than likely be aware of that (after all, they do it too!). But if you choose an intriguing wine or other drink to serve with it – one that is not only interesting in its own right but heightens the flavour of the food, then you'll have created an experience to remember.

The beauty of this approach is that you don't have to be an experienced cook to pull it off. You simply need to develop a flair for what ingredients work well together, just as those who dress stylishly can put together a 'look' or others can make their house look great by the colours and furnishings they choose.

This book is very much written with the pressures of modern life in mind. We want to show our friends hospitality, but we simply don't have time in our busy days to make everything from scratch. So we need to be more imaginative and flexible about the way we do it.

Don't feel duty bound to offer a full meal. Sure, it's fun occasionally to throw a full-blown dinner party such as my Fine Wine Dinner (see page 130), but it's equally enjoyable to just invite friends round for a few tapas (see page 66) or for margaritas and a few tostaditas (see page 62). Or ask them to come round after dinner for an indulgent pudding and a glass of sweet wine (see Just Desserts on page 140). They'll love the novelty and, faced with far less work in the kitchen, so will you!

Why not try reflecting the seasons in your choice of food and drink. You'll also make life easier for yourself and more enjoyable for your guests. Let local food growers and producers inspire you with the first of the new season's organic vegetables and throw together a Farmers' Market Supper (see page 78). At the end of the year, make an old-fashioned Vegetarian Harvest Supper (see page 96) with the pick of the autumn's produce.

When the weather hots up, take your lead from those who live year-round in a tropical climate and serve spicy but cooling food (see page 72). When temperatures hit zero, stay indoors and huddle up around the comforting sort of fare I've suggested in my It's Cold Outside menu (see page 102). Even the cheeseboards you serve your guests can be given an imaginative seasonal twist, as you'll see from my ideas on pages 136–139.

I suggest that you use the menus and ideas in this book as a starting point for a new style of entertaining at home – one where the idea comes first, then you invite friends round to share the experience, rather than inviting them round then desperately wondering what to cook for them.

Cook if you feel like it, buy in food if you really don't. Use interesting and carefully chosen drinks – beers, cocktails, juices and liqueurs – as well as wine, to make your meals special. Most importantly, relax and enjoy!

the secrets of successful entertaining

For many people entertaining is stressful: something to be crammed into an already hectic life. We invite friends, work colleagues or neighbours round on impulse, then wish we hadn't. We leave thinking about the event until the last minute, try something too complicated, then panic. But it really doesn't need to be like that. Just follow these simple tips and enjoy rather than endure the events you host:

DO

• Match the occasion to the guests...

There's no point in inviting older family members or friends to a noisy stand-up drinks party where they struggle to hear who they're talking to. They'd much rather be seated in a smaller group round the table. Younger friends on the other hand will be perfectly happy to eat finger food and perch a plate on their knee.

• ...and the time of year.

Seasonal food is so much more inviting – light, fresh food in the summer warm, comforting food when it's miserable and cold. Have a Plan B if it's an outdoor event – you can never be a hundred per cent sure of the weather.

• Plan ahead. Make a couple of dishes in advance and freeze them. Make sure you have the equipment you need, especially if you're catering for a crowd (see page 147). Draw up a full shopping list and get as much as possible done the day beforehand.

• Rope in friends to help. If they offer to help with the cooking, accept gratefully – letting them know the kind of dish you'd like if there's a theme to the event. If there's a task to be done on the day – barbecuing, juicing, making margaritas – get them involved.

• If you cheat (as we all do from time to time), cheat in style! Pretty-up bought food and give it a personal touch, adding fresh herbs, for example, or a squeeze of lemon.

• Lay on plenty of water and other soft drinks in addition to the alcohol.

DON'T

• Invite people you don't know too well for a long evening. Ask them round for drinks so they can stay for as long, or as short, a time as they like and talk to a range of people.

• Host a huge party if organization isn't your strong suit. Hold two or three smaller events rather than one big one or get it catered by someone else

• Feel guilty about not making every single thing yourself. The menus that follow in this book contain dishes that will work well together, but you can always buy a similar dish.

• Tackle a complicated recipe you've never made before. If you feel unsure about it, try it out on the family first. Never attempt a whole menu of untried dishes if you're not a confident cook.

• Worry about impressing your guests. Your friends come to see you, not to judge how your table is decorated or how good a cook you are – at least that's what real friends do. If you have to offer hospitality to someone who stresses you out, invite them to a restaurant rather than to your home.

• Spend all your time locked away in the kitchen or jumping up and down at the table. Get ahead, then relax and enjoy yourself on the day. (There's no point in entertaining if you don't!)

• Top up glasses too regularly. Both you and your guests will feel uncomfortable if they drink too much.

food and wine matching made easy

If you've ever tasted a food you love with a wine that matches it perfectly, you'll know that the combination of the two can be even better than the food and wine on its own. But how to find those perfect pairings? The old 'white wine with fish, red wine with meat' rule is a bit dated, as anyone who has enjoyed a seared tuna steak with a Pinot Noir well knows. Wine has changed. Food has changed. The only rule is that there are no hard and fast rules, just combinations that most people are likely to enjoy.

Basically, there's no great mystique about it. Simply use your existing knowledge of food and think of wine as another ingredient you have to take into account when you're planning a meal – rather as you would when you choose a vegetable or sauce to serve on the side. The more food and wine matches you try, the more confident you'll feel, so take every opportunity to try out different combinations, particularly in restaurants that serve wines by the glass or suggest food and wine pairings with their menu. Here are some simple pointers that may help you:

• Match the wine to the sauce, not the basic ingredient. Chicken, for example, can be cooked in any number of different ways, so it's more useful to think about whether it's served in a creamy white wine and mushroom sauce (a smooth, dry white), a red wine sauce like *coq au vin* (a similar wine to the one you use to cook it), a Thai green curry sauce (a fruity, off-dry white) or a barbecue sauce or marinade (a ripe, fruity red).

• Think about the temperature and intensity of the dish. Dishes that are served raw or delicate, steamed dishes need lighter wines (usually white) than ones that are roasted, seared or grilled (more often red). Homemade dishes will often be more intensely seasoned than bought ones, so may need more intensely flavoured wines.

• Take into account what else is on the plate. Strongly flavoured vegetables, such as asparagus, red cabbage or beetroot or fruity salsas and relishes, can make a difference to the wine you choose. If you served grilled salmon with asparagus, for instance, you'd probably go for a Sauvignon Blanc, while if you made a spicy mango salsa to go with it, go for a Semillion or Semillion-Chardonnay, or a fruity red.

• If you're serving several wines during a meal, you should generally start with lighter, drier wines and move on to richer, more full-bodied ones. Usually, that means white followed by red, but you could easily serve a full-bodied white with a main course or a lighter red followed by a more full-bodied one.

• Dessert wines need to be sweeter than the food they're accompanying, otherwise they can taste sharp.

• Stuck? Imagine wine as a fruit. If it's light and citrussy, it will go with dishes where you might think of adding a squeeze of lemon as you would to fried fish or chicken. If it has ripe red berry fruit flavours, it will probably go with ingredients to which you might think of adding red fruits such as duck, turkey or lamb.

For more information on this topic, see Matching Wine to Food (page 150) and Matching Food to Wine (page 153) or look at my website www.matchingfoodandwine.com.

the menus

friends for brunch

menu for 6

At weekends it's good to change the usual workday routine of breakfast and lunch and offer brunch, especially if you have guests staying over. The food needs to be light and fresh but flavourful, healthy but comforting. A main course of kedgeree is easier than juggling a fry-up for a crowd, while the muffins can be made in advance, frozen and lightly reheated. And the juice bar makes a fun focus to the occasion.

Bloody Mary granitas

summer berries with Greek yoghurt, honey and granola

smoked salmon kedgeree

mini-muffins:
banana and honey; bacon, onion and Cheddar;
courgette, goats' cheese and spring onion

'Juice Bar'
St. Clement's punch, strawberry sunrise

TO DRINK: Sparkling wine is the best wine to serve at a brunch: it suits the time of day perfectly and is a great match with eggs. Unless it's a special occasion, it needn't be Champagne: there are many good quality sparkling wines from Australia, California and New Zealand. You can serve it straight or mix it half and half with fresh orange juice for a refreshing Bucks Fizz. I'd also lay on a few beers (golden lagers or wheat beers) for those who prefer beer to wine.

Bloody Mary granitas

A refreshing palate cleanser to kick off or round up brunch.

7–8 tomatoes, skinned and roughly chopped

450 ml tomato juice

100 ml vodka

1 tablespoon Worcestershire sauce

freshly squeezed juice of 1 lime

1 teaspoon celery salt

1 teaspoon finely grated onion

sea salt, freshly ground black pepper and hot pepper sauce, such as Tabasco, to taste

a few finely snipped chives, to garnish

Makes 10–12 shots

Put the tomatoes in a food processor and whizz until smooth. Add the tomato juice and vodka and whizz again. Next, add the Worcestershire sauce, lime juice, celery salt and onion, whizz, then check the seasoning, adding salt, pepper and hot pepper sauce to taste. Pour into a shallow plastic box and freeze for about 1½ hours. Rough up the surface with a fork and freeze for another 45 minutes. Fork through again and freeze for another 45 minutes if serving straight away or freeze until hard if making ahead, in which case mellow in the fridge for 30 minutes before serving.

Spoon into shot glasses and garnish with a few finely snipped chives. Serve with coffee spoons or other small spoons.

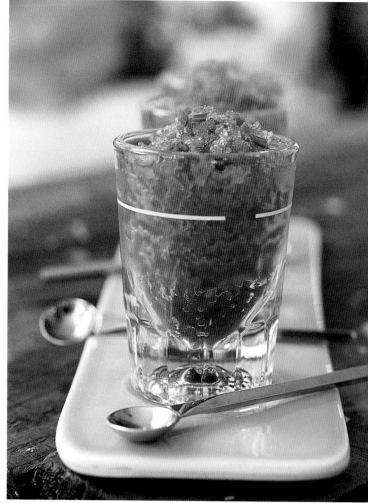

summer berries with Greek yoghurt, honey and granola

Fill a large glass bowl with assorted fresh berries such as strawberries, raspberries, blueberries and stoned cherries. Have a big bowl of Greek or Greek-style yoghurt and a smaller one of Greek honey or other flavoured clear honey alongside, together with a bowl of crunchy granola.

smoked salmon kedgeree

Kedgeree is an Anglo-Indian dish that stems from the days of the Raj. This party version is based on a relatively new product – lightly smoked salmon, which gives it a particularly luxurious flavour. If you can't find it, use organic salmon and add a little bit of smoked salmon at the end when you add the prawns.

3 large eggs

250 g undyed skinless, smoked haddock or cod fillet

250 g lightly smoked skinless, salmon fillet or ordinary salmon fillet

3 tablespoons sunflower oil

1 onion, finely chopped

2–3 teaspoons mild curry powder

300 g basmati rice

175 g cooked shelled prawns

40 g butter, softened

2–3 tablespoons freshly squeezed lemon juice

3 heaped tablespoons chopped coriander leaves, plus a few whole leaves to garnish

sea salt and freshly ground black pepper

Serves 6

Bring a small saucepan of water to the boil. Prick the eggs if you have an egg pricker, lower them carefully into the water and boil for 10–12 minutes. Drain off the water, pour cold running water over the eggs, then leave to cool in cold water.

Put the smoked haddock and salmon into a large saucepan and pour over just enough cold water to cover. Bring gradually to the boil, then once the water is bubbling, take the pan off the heat and cover it with a lid or a piece of foil. Leave for 5 minutes, then carefully remove the fish fillets. Pour the cooking water into a jug up to the 600 ml mark and set aside.

Heat the oil in another heavy-duty pan or flameproof casserole and fry the onion over moderate heat for about 6–7 minutes until starting to turn dark brown at the edges. Sprinkle in the curry powder (I use 3 teaspoons, but use 2 if you want a slightly milder flavour). Add the rice, stir again and pour in the reserved water you used for cooking the fish. Bring to the boil then turn the heat right down and cover the pan. Cook for about 15–20 minutes until all the liquid has been absorbed.

Meanwhile, shell and quarter the eggs. Set aside 6 quarters and roughly chop the rest. Flake the fish, being very careful to remove any remaining bones. Once the rice is cooked, fork it through and tip in the cooked fish, prawns and chopped eggs, cover the pan and leave for 5 minutes over very low heat. Turn off the heat, add the butter, fork through. Season to taste with the lemon juice and a little salt and pepper if you think it needs it and fork through the chopped coriander. Serve on a warmed platter garnished with the quartered eggs and the remaining coriander leaves.

* You can keep the kedgeree warm in a covered pan for about 15–20 minutes before serving or transfer it to a very low oven for about 30–40 minutes.

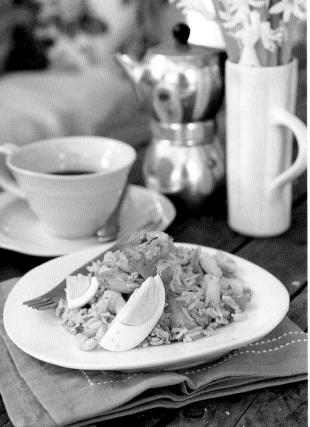

breakfast muffins

banana and honey mini-muffins

50 g unsalted butter
2 tablespoons clear honey
1 heaped tablespoon natural yoghurt
about 60 ml milk
½ teaspoon vanilla extract
150 g plain flour
1½ teaspoons baking powder
½ teaspoon ground cinnamon
¼ teaspoon salt
1 large egg, lightly beaten
1 medium-ripe banana
unrefined caster sugar, for topping

a 12-hole small muffin or tartlet tin
12 small paper cases

Makes about 12 small muffins

Preheat the oven to 190°C (375°F) Gas 5. Line the hollows in the tin with the paper cases. Gently heat the butter in a saucepan with the honey. Set aside and cool slightly. Put the yoghurt in a measuring jug and mix in enough milk to bring it to just over the 100 ml mark. Stir in the vanilla extract. Sift the flour into a bowl with the baking powder, cinnamon and salt and hollow out a dip in the centre. Pour the honey and butter mixture, beaten egg and yoghurt and milk into the flour and mix in lightly and swiftly with a large metal spoon to get a rough batter. (Don't overmix – it doesn't have to be completely smooth). Peel the banana, slice it thinly into the batter and fold in lightly so that all the slices are coated. Spoon the batter into the muffin cases and sprinkle each with a little caster sugar. Bake for about 20 minutes or until fully risen and well browned. Transfer to a wire rack and eat as soon as cool enough to handle.

bacon, onion and Cheddar mini-muffins

1 tablespoon sunflower or other cooking oil
75 g cubed pancetta or bacon lardons
1 small onion, finely chopped
50 g unsalted butter
1 heaped tablespoon natural yoghurt
about 60 ml milk
150 g plain flour
1½ teaspoons baking powder
¼ teaspoon salt
15 g finely grated Parmesan cheese
1 large egg, lightly beaten
40 g coarsely grated Cheddar cheese

a 12-hole small muffin or tartlet tin
12 small paper cases

Makes about 12 small muffins

Preheat the oven to 190°C (375°F) Gas 5. Line the hollows in the tin with the paper cases. Heat the oil in a small frying pan and fry the bacon for a couple of minutes until it starts to brown. Add the onion, stir and cook over low to medium heat for another 5 minutes until the onion is soft, then set aside to cool. Gently melt the butter in another pan and leave to cool. Put the yoghurt in a measuring jug and mix in enough milk to bring it to just over the 100 ml mark. Sift the flour into a bowl with the baking powder and salt. Add the Parmesan and hollow out a dip in the centre. Pour the beaten egg, melted butter and yoghurt and milk into the flour and mix in lightly and swiftly with a large metal spoon to get a rough batter. (Don't overmix – it doesn't have to be completely smooth). Fold in the bacon and onion. Spoon the batter into the muffin cases and sprinkle each with a little grated Cheddar. Bake for 20–25 minutes or until fully risen and well browned. Transfer to a wire rack and eat as soon as cool enough to handle.

courgette, goats' cheese and spring onion mini-muffins

Follow the Bacon, Onion and Cheddar Mini-Muffin recipe substituting 75 g grated courgette, 75 g grated mature goats' cheese and 1–2 trimmed and thinly sliced spring onion for the bacon, onion and Cheddar. (You don't need to precook the courgette and onion, so you don't need the oil either.) Again, save some of the cheese for topping the muffins.

You could also add a tablespoon of finely chopped dill to the mixture. I think these are better served cold rather than warm.

juice bar

It's fun to give your guests a chance to make their own juices and smoothies. Just lay on a selection of different fruits and a blender or juicer. Combinations that go well are all kinds of citrus fruits; strawberries, orange and banana; and carrot, apple, lemon and ginger. (See also Watermelon and Strawberry cooler page 49.)

Time-saving tip:

If you don't have a juicer, buy high-quality ready-made chilled juices or smoothies and serve them in attractive glass jugs.

St. Clement's punch

This is a fresh, zesty, citrus-based punch that's packed with vitamin C.

250 ml freshly squeezed orange juice (about 4 oranges)
150 ml freshly squeezed pink grapefruit juice (1–2 grapefruit)
250 ml lemon refresher or traditional lemonade, chilled
slices of orange and lemon, to garnish

Serves 4–6

Simply pour the orange and pink grapefruit juice into a jug, top up with the lemon refresher and stir well. Add a few slices of orange and lemon to the jug and serve.

* If you're feeling indulgent, simply add a tablespoon of Grand Marnier. It just gives it that extra edge!

strawberry sunrise

Technically, this is a smoothie (a mixture of fruit juice and yoghurt) rather than a juice and can be made in an ordinary blender. Ideal for those who can't face solid food until lunchtime.

2 ripe bananas
200 g fresh strawberries
freshly squeezed juice of 2 oranges
300 ml natural yoghurt
clear honey, to taste

Serves 2–3

Peel and slice the banana. Hull and halve the strawberries. Place both in a blender goblet with the juice of 1 orange and whizz until smooth. Add the yoghurt and honey to taste and whizz again.

an Italian al fresco lunch

menu for 6

Combine an Italian menu with eating out of doors, and you have a guaranteed formula for happy guests. It's easy on the cook too. The Ham and Melon Platter couldn't be simpler to put together and, with its pale green, orange and pink colours, makes a strikingly pretty plate to bring to the table. The Grape and Mascarpone Tart takes very little time to assemble – so all you have to do is keep an eye on your typically Tuscan-style roast. You can keep the Italian theme going with the drinks you serve.

ham and melon platter

TO DRINK Cinzano Bianco and soda (see p.23) – (its sweetness and delicate herbal notes will work perfectly.)

Tuscan-style roast veal and wild mushrooms

with roast new potatoes and buttered spinach

TO DRINK   An elegant Chianti Classico Riserva.

grape and lemon mascarpone tart

TO DRINK A glass of gently sparkling honeysuckle sweet Moscato d'Asti, served well chilled in Champagne flutes.

ham and melon platter

For colour contrast you need an orange Canteloupe or Charentais melon and a green Galia, Ogen or Honeydew melon, and some thinly sliced Parma ham and prosciutto cotto all'erbe. Quarter and deseed the melons, cut the wedges off the skin, then cut them into thick slices. Arrange on a big plate along with loosely draped slices of ham. The platter wants to look quite casual – lavish and generous, rather than arranged into perfectly lined up rows.

Serve the platter with some olive breadsticks and mini ciabattas, refreshed in the oven.

Italian aperitivos

Like the French, the Italians have a huge range of bittersweet aperitifs or aperitivos to get the tastebuds going including such drinks as Campari, Cinzano and Aperol. Though less fashionable than they once were, they can be delicious with food and are refreshingly low in alcohol.

To make a Cinzano and soda (pictured left), put 4–5 ice cubes in a glass, fill half to two-thirds of the way up with Cinzano Bianco and top up with chilled soda water.

The charming Venetian sparkling wine Prosecco also makes a fine aperitivo. Mix it with freshly pressed peach juice for a classic Bellini cocktail.

Tuscan-style roast veal with wild mushrooms

I ate a dish like this at Castello di Brolio in Tuscany and couldn't wait till I got home to recreate it. It's a brilliant dish to match with wine – light but intensely flavourful – the perfect partner for a Chianti Classico Riserva.

1 kg boned, rolled loin or rack of veal or pork (ask the butcher to give you the bones)
3 tablespoons olive oil
50 g butter
1 onion, cut into 8
1 large carrot, cut into chunks
3 large garlic cloves, peeled and quartered
3 sprigs of rosemary
250 ml dry Italian white wine
250 ml fresh chicken stock or light vegetable stock made with ½ organic stock cube
150 g wild mushrooms
1 dessertspoon plain flour
a few drops of Marsala or sweet sherry (optional)
sea salt and freshly ground black pepper

a large, deep, lidded and flameproof casserole

Serves 6

Preheat the oven to 200°C (400°F) Gas 6. Pat the veal dry and season all over with salt and pepper. Put the casserole over medium heat, add 1½ tablespoons of the olive oil, heat for a minute, then add 15 g of the butter. When the foaming dies down, put in the veal, bones, onion and carrot and brown on all sides, turning regularly.

Add the garlic and rosemary to the casserole, stir and add 3 tablespoons of the white wine. Cover with a lid and transfer to the oven. Roast for about 2 hours. Check occasionally that the meat and vegetables aren't burning and add a little more white wine if necessary.

Remove the veal from the casserole and set aside on a warmed carving plate. Cover lightly with foil and leave to rest for at least half an hour.

Pour off any surface fat from the juices in the casserole, then add the remaining white wine and bring to the boil, working in the tasty caramelized juices stuck on the side of the casserole. Simmer and reduce the liquid by half, then add half the stock and simmer for another 10 minutes. Strain through a fine sieve.

Heat the remaining butter in a small frying pan and fry the mushrooms until the butter and any liquid have almost evaporated. Stir in the flour. Pour in the strained stock, bring to the boil and simmer for 5 minutes. Add a little more stock if the sauce seems too thick. Check the seasoning, add salt and pepper to taste and a dash of Marsala if you like a touch of sweetness.

For a rack of veal, offer the sauce separately, otherwise finely slice the meat, arrange on a warmed platter and spoon over the sauce. Serve with roast new potatoes and buttered spinach (see right).

roast new potatoes with olive oil

3 tablespoons olive oil
750–800 g baby new potatoes, washed and dried
sea salt and freshly ground black pepper

Serves 6

Preheat the oven to 200°C (400°F) Gas 6 (if not already on for the meat). Measure the oil into a shallow roasting tin, tip in the potatoes and shake the tin so that they get evenly covered with oil. Put the pan in the oven and roast for about 35–40 minutes until the potatoes are nicely browned, turning them halfway through. Season lightly with salt and pepper.

buttered spinach

750 g loose spinach leaves
2 tablespoons extra virgin olive oil
25 g butter
sea salt and freshly ground black pepper
freshly grated nutmeg, to taste

Serves 6

Tip the leaves into a sinkful of cold water and give them a good swirl. Discard any damaged leaves and remove the central tough rib from the larger leaves. Drain and pack into a large saucepan without any extra water. Put the pan over low heat, cover and leave for about 5 minutes. Turn the leaves over (the bottom leaves should have collapsed). Re-cover and cook for another 3–4 minutes until all the leaves have collapsed but are still bright green. Drain thoroughly in a colander pressing out the excess water. Return the leaves to the pan and chop roughly. Add the oil and butter and heat until the spinach is hot and the butter melted. Season to taste with salt, pepper and nutmeg.

grape and lemon mascarpone tart

This is a really simple dessert that you can make with a ready-rolled pastry base. A gorgeous Italian lemon liqueur gives a sharp edge to the creamy mascarpone.

230 g ready-rolled puff pastry, thawed if frozen

2 large organic eggs, separated

2 tablespoons unrefined caster sugar, plus 1 teaspoon for sprinkling

250-g tub mascarpone cheese

2½ tablespoons Limoncello (lemon liqueur)

250 g white seedless or halved and seeded grapes, rinsed and dried

250 g red seedless or halved and seeded grapes, rinsed and dried

1 teaspoon icing sugar

a large, square or rectangular baking tray, lightly greased

Serves 6–8

Preheat the oven to 200°C (400°F) Gas 6.

Take the pastry out of the fridge and let it rest for 20 minutes. Unroll and lift carefully onto the baking tray. Trim around the edge to make a 28-cm round.

Lightly whisk the egg whites and brush a thin layer onto the pastry. Sprinkle with 1 teaspoon sugar, then use a fork to prick the pastry all over. Bake for 10–12 minutes until puffy and brown. Leave to cool while you make the topping.

Tip the mascarpone cheese into a bowl and gradually work in the Limoncello. Using an electric hand-held whisk, beat the egg yolks with the remaining caster sugar until pale, thick and creamy. Gently fold the mascarpone mixture into the eggs until thoroughly blended.

Transfer the cooled pastry base to a large serving plate or tray. Spread over the mascarpone mixture with a spatula, taking it almost up to the edges. Scatter the grapes on top to get a nice mix of colours.

Sift over the icing sugar and serve straight away, or chill the tart for a couple of hours, then sprinkle with icing sugar when ready to serve.

a Provençal-style lunch

menu for 6

If you want to entertain friends in summer, what could be more appealing than a light, flavourful Mediterranean lunch? Start with a cool, refreshing pastis or a glass of rosé and some typically Provençal olive-based nibbles, then serve some simply seared tuna – cooked on the barbecue if you feel like firing it up. Finally, a classic apricot tart with a twist, flavoured with the gorgeous southern French dessert wine, Muscat de Beaumes-de-Venise. Simple and stylish.

❧

anchovy and green olive dip with ciabatta toasts
mini pissaladières

TO DRINK Pastis or a chilled dry rosé. Dilute pastis (I like Henri Bardouin) about 1:5 with cool (not iced) water. Serve in small tumblers.

seared tuna with tomatoes, rocket and gremolata

TO DRINK The rosé will also go with the tuna.

apricot tart with Muscat de Beaumes-de-Venise

TO DRINK Muscat de Beaumes-de-Venise.

anchovy and green olive dip

This is one of the easiest dips or spreads you can make.

100-g jar anchovy fillets marinated in olive oil
with garlic and herbs*
25 g pitted green olives
75 ml Provençal or Spanish olive oil
1 tablespoon red wine vinegar
2–3 tablespoons warm water
freshly ground black pepper

For the topping:
50 g pitted green olives
3 tablespoons chopped flat leaf parsley
ciabatta toasts (see right) to serve
a selection of crudités (radishes, carrot and
fennel strips) to serve

Serves 6

Tip the anchovies and their oil into a food processor with the olives
and whizz until smooth. Gradually add the olive oil until you have
a mayonnaise-type consistency. Add the red wine vinegar and
sufficient warm water to make a spreadable consistency. Season
with black pepper.

Chop the remaining olives and parsley together for the topping.
Spread the anchovy paste thinly over the toasts and spoon over a
little of the green olive topping. Serve on a platter decorated with
radishes, carrot sticks and fennel strips.

* If you can't find marinated anchovies, buy ordinary anchovies in
olive oil and add 1 garlic clove and 1 tablespoon finely chopped
parsley to the mixture.

Time-saving tip: You could also spread some of the toasts with
ready-made tapénade (a purée of capers, black olives, anchovies
and olive oil).

ciabatta toasts

It's worth making a large batch of these, as they keep well.

2 ready-to-bake ciabatta loaves
olive oil spray or 4–6 tablespoons light olive oil

2 baking trays

Makes about 30–32 slices

Preheat the oven to 180°C (350°F) Gas 4. Cut the ciabatta on the
slant into fairly thin slices. Spray both sides with olive oil or pour
the olive oil on the baking trays and dip the slices of ciabatta in it.
Bake for 15 minutes, turning the slices halfway through. Repeat
with any remaining ciabatta slices. Cool, then store the toasts in
an airtight tin.

mini pissaladières

For the topping:

2 tablespoons olive oil

2 large sweet onions (about 500 g in total), thinly sliced

1 garlic clove, finely chopped

1 teaspoon finely chopped thyme or ½ teaspoon dried thyme

150 g small pitted marinated black olives

sea salt and freshly ground black pepper

a few small basil leaves, to garnish

For the pastry:

100 g Quark or curd cheese

100 g butter, cut into cubes

125 g plain flour

1 teaspoon baking powder

a good pinch of salt

an 8-cm pastry cutter
2 x 12-hole shallow tartlet tins

Makes about 12–14

Heat the oil in a large flameproof casserole or saucepan. Tip in the onions, then cook over a medium heat until they have begun to collapse (about 10 minutes). Stir in the garlic and thyme, turn the heat down a little and continue to cook for another 30–40 minutes until the onions are soft and golden and any liquid has evaporated, taking care that they don't catch and burn. Season with salt and pepper and set aside to cool.

While the onions are cooking, make the pastry. Tip the Quark into a food processor with the softened butter and process until smooth. Sift the flour with the baking powder and salt and add to the creamed cheese and butter in 2 batches, using the pulse to incorporate it. Once the mixture starts to form a ball, turn it out of the processor onto a floured board and form it into a flat disc. Put it in a plastic bag and chill for an hour in the fridge.

When ready to cook the tartlets, heat the oven to 220°C (425°F) Gas 7. Roll out the pastry quite thinly. Stamp rounds out of the pastry, re-rolling the offcuts as necessary, and lay them in the hollows of the tartlet tins. Spoon in teaspoonfuls of the cooled onion mixture and top with an olive. Bake for 15–20 minutes until the pastry is puffed up and golden. Cool for 10 minutes, then remove the tarts carefully from the tin and arrange on a plate. Scatter with a few small basil leaves and serve. You can bake and freeze these, then reheat them from frozen in a moderate oven.

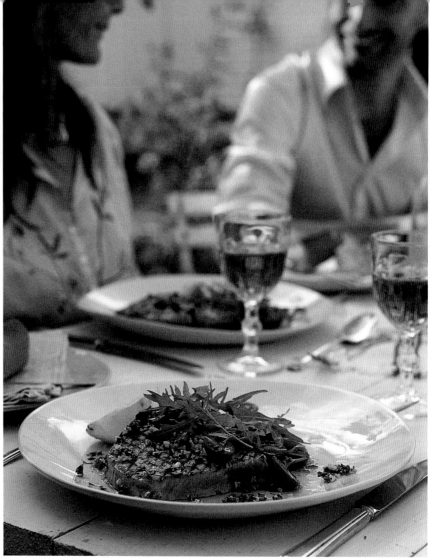

2 unwaxed lemons

3 large garlic cloves

40 g parsley

2 rounded tablespoons capers, rinsed if salted

6 fresh tuna steaks, about 150 g each

350 g pomodorino or other cherry tomatoes

100 g wild rocket

sea salt and freshly ground black pepper

extra virgin olive oil, to drizzle

Serves 6

seared tuna with tomatoes, rocket and gremolata

This simple dish can equally well be adapted to a conventional grill or a barbecue.*

First make the gremolata. Grate the zest finely from the lemons, taking care not to remove too much white pith. Peel the garlic cloves and chop them finely. Take the tough ends off the parsley stalks and finely chop the leaves. Roughly chop the capers, then pull all the ingredients together on the chopping board and chop them together to mix them thoroughly. Set aside in a bowl. Quarter the lemons.

When you're ready to cook, heat a ridged grill pan or frying pan until almost smoking (about 3 minutes). Rub both sides of the tuna steaks with olive oil and season with sea salt rubbed between your fingers and black pepper. Lay as many tuna steaks as you can fit in the pan and cook for about 1½–2 minutes, depending on the thickness and how rare you like them. Turn them over and cook the other side for 1–1½ minutes. Set aside on a warmed serving dish and cover lightly with foil. Repeat with the remaining tuna steaks. Rinse the pan under hot running water, dry with kitchen paper and reheat until very hot. Add 2 tablespoons oil and tip in the tomatoes. Cook for 1–1½ minutes, shaking the pan till the skins start to split then turn off the heat. To serve, put a small handful of rocket on each plate, top with a few tomatoes and lay the tuna steaks alongside. Drizzle the tuna and salad with olive oil and a good squeeze of lemon juice, and sprinkle over the gremolata. Serve with some authentic French crusty baguette.

* If you use the grill or barbecue to cook the tuna, just sauté the tomatoes quickly in a frying pan to serve with the salad.

apricot tart with Muscat de Beaumes-de-Venise

This is my version of a brilliantly simple recipe from award-winning food writer Alastair Hendy. If you've never made a tart in your life, you could make this.

375-g pack ready-rolled puff pastry, thawed if frozen
750 g ripe apricots
2 tablespoons ground almonds
2 tablespoons unrefined caster sugar
2 tablespoons Muscat de Beaumes-de-Venise
3 tablespoons soft-set apricot jam
Greek yoghurt or vanilla ice cream, to serve

a shallow, rectangular, non-stick baking tin

Serves 6

Preheat the oven to 225°C (425°F) Gas 7 and take the pastry out of the fridge about 10 minutes before you want to unroll it.

Halve and stone the apricots (you can cut the bigger ones into thirds). Unroll the pastry and lay it on the baking tin, trimming off any pastry that overhangs the edges. Prick the base with the prongs of a fork and shake over the ground almonds in an even layer. Sprinkle over 1 tablespoon of the sugar. Arrange the apricot halves or thirds in rows over the surface of the tart, leaving a narrow border around the edge and propping up each row on the one behind it. Spoon over the remaining sugar. Bake in the preheated oven for 30–35 minutes until the pastry is risen and the edges of the fruit are beginning to caramelize.

Spoon the jam into a small saucepan, add the Muscat and warm gently over low heat, stirring until smooth. Brush the warm glaze over the apricots and serve the tart with double cream or vanilla ice cream.

a summer picnic

menu for 6

Picnic food doesn't have to be rough and ready, as this sophisticated menu shows. Get ahead by making the Sun-dried Tomato, Olive and Basil Bread, Lavender Shortbread and Homemade Lemonade in advance, leaving you only the Chicken Tonnato Pasta Salad to assemble on the day (watch out – everyone is going to want the recipe!) Short of time? The menu is easy to adapt to a deli-bought meal. Just buy a nice quiche, some ready-made shortbread and some of the lovely lemonades that are now available.

sun-dried tomato, olive and basil bread with
handcut salami

chicken tonnato pasta salad

fresh peaches and cherries with lavender shortbread

homemade lemonade

TO DRINK Rosé is the perfect wine for this summery menu. I'd suggest a drier style from southern France or Spain (where it is called rosado), but if you prefer the fuller, fruitier New World style that is more like a light red, by all means go for it. The important thing is to keep it cold. Chill well beforehand and transport in insulated bags.

sun-dried tomato, olive and basil bread

175 g plain flour

1 tablespoon baking powder

3 large eggs

100 ml long-life milk

100 ml olive oil

100 g mature Gruyère cheese, grated

100 g sun-dried tomatoes in oil*, drained and roughly chopped

60 g pitted black olives marinated with herbs, roughly chopped

a small handful of basil leaves, roughly sliced

sea salt and freshly ground black pepper

a 21 x 11-cm rectangular, non-stick loaf tin, lightly greased and floured

Serves 6

These easy breads are very popular in France where they somewhat confusingly call them 'cake'. They're like a cross between a savoury bread and a quiche, and delicious to nibble with drinks.

Preheat the oven to 180°C (350°F) Gas 4. Sift the flour with the baking powder and season well with salt and black pepper. Whisk the eggs and whisk in the milk and oil. Tip two-thirds of the liquid into the flour, beat well, then add the remaining liquid. Mix in the Gruyère, tomatoes, olives and basil, then tip into the prepared loaf tin. Bake in the preheated oven for 50 minutes or until a skewer comes out clean. Cool, then remove from the tin. Wrap in foil and keep in the fridge. Serve at room temperature, sliced and cut into halves or squares. You could also serve a plate of some chunky handcut, slices of salami that can be eaten with your fingers.

* If the sun-dried tomatoes come in oil, use a couple of tablespoons of the tomato-flavoured oil to replace the olive oil in this recipe.

chicken tonnato pasta salad

This is a really easy yet impressive pasta salad. Don't be daunted by the rather long list of ingredients – the gremolata is based on pretty well the same ingredients as the sauce, but simply chopped rough for added texture.

500 ml fresh chicken stock or made with 1 organic stock cube

250 ml dry white wine

1 small onion, sliced

1 celery stick, trimmed and cut into 3 pieces

1 bay leaf

2 slices of unwaxed lemon

8–10 black peppercorns

4 skinless, boneless chicken breasts (about 600 g in total)

200 g dried egg pasta shapes, such as Campanelle

8 halved, grilled artichoke hearts (optional)

1 tablespoon roughly chopped flat leaf parsley

For the dressing:

100 g premium (preferably Spanish) tuna, drained of oil

2 tablespoons small capers, rinsed

about 2 tablespoons freshly squeezed lemon juice

3 canned or bottled anchovy fillets, rinsed and finely chopped

200 g good-quality mayonnaise

a pinch of cayenne pepper

For the gremolata:

5–6 canned or bottled anchovy fillets, rinsed and chopped

2 spring onions, trimmed and thinly sliced

grated zest of 1 small unwaxed lemon or ½ large one

1 tablespoon small capers

3 tablespoons chopped flat leaf parsley

Also pack:

3 Little Gem lettuces, washed and crisped in the fridge, or a bag of mixed salad leaves or rocket

500 g cherry tomatoes

a small bottle of olive oil

Serves 6

Pour the stock and wine into a large saucepan, big enough to take the chicken breasts in a single layer. Bring to the boil, add the onion, celery, bay leaf, lemon and peppercorns and simmer for 5 minutes. Carefully lower the chicken breasts into the stock, adding some boiling water, if needed, to cover them. Bring back to the boil, then turn the heat right down and simmer very slowly for another 5 minutes. Turn the heat off, cover the pan and let the chicken cool in the stock. (This will take about 4–5 hours.)

Once the chicken is cool, make the dressing. Put the drained tuna in a food processor with the capers, lemon juice and anchovy fillets and whizz until you have a paste. Add the mayonnaise and cayenne pepper and whizz again until smooth. Turn into a large bowl. Put all the ingredients for the gremolata on a chopping board and chop them together.

Cook the pasta following the instructions on the packet and refresh with cold water.

Remove the chicken from the poaching liquid and cut into rough chunks. Add the chicken, pasta and gremolata to the dressing and toss lightly. Check the seasoning, adding more lemon juice or cayenne pepper to taste if you think it needs it (you shouldn't need salt). Transfer to a large plastic box, arrange the artichoke hearts, if using, over the top and sprinkle with parsley.

To assemble, arrange a handful of salad leaves on each plate, scatter over a few tomatoes, drizzle over a little olive oil, then spoon the salad on top. Serve with some crusty bread.

homemade lemonade

You will need a juicer to make this absolutely delicious lemonade – in fact, it's almost worth buying one just to make it.

150 g unrefined caster sugar
4 large juicy unwaxed lemons, plus 1 extra, sliced, to garnish
1 litre still or sparkling mineral water, chilled
a few sprigs of mint
plenty of ice, to serve

Makes 6–8 glasses

Put the sugar in a saucepan with 150 ml water. Heat over low heat, stirring until the sugar has completely dissolved, then bring to the boil and boil for 5 minutes without stirring. Take off the heat and leave to cool. Cut 2 of the lemons into small chunks and pass through the feeder tube of a juicer. They should produce about 150 ml thick juice. Squeeze the remaining lemons (again, that should yield about 150 ml) and add to the other juice. Stir in the sugar syrup you've made.

Chill the lemon concentrate until ready to use. Either pour into a large jugful of ice and pour in an equal amount of chilled still or sparkling mineral water or pour a couple of shots of lemonade into a tumbler full of ice and top up with chilled mineral water. Garnish with lemon slices and sprigs of mint

Variation:

Raspberry lemonade

Purée (in a food processor or force through a nylon sieve) 150 g of fresh or frozen raspberries and sweeten with 2 tablespoons sugar syrup (see recipe above). Stir into the lemonade base and dilute as described. Decorate with lemon slices and a few whole raspberries.

lavender shortbread

Homemade shortbread is unbelievably easy to make. Cornflour will make it smoother; ground rice or fine semolina more crumbly and rustic.

Preheat the oven to 150°F (300°C) Gas 2. Put the sugar and butter in a food processor and process until light and fluffy (or beat together with an electric hand-held whisk). Add the lavender essence or flowers and whizz again. Add half the flour and pulse to incorporate, then add the remaining flour and pulse again. Add the cornflour and pulse again until incorporated. (Or add in stages, by hand, beating with a wooden spoon then bring the mixture together with your hands). Tip the mixture into a baking tin and spread out until even. Mark the shortbread with a sharp knife, dividing it into 18 squares, and prick lightly with the prongs of a fork. Bake in the preheated oven for about 40–45 minutes until pale gold in colour. Sprinkle with the remaining sugar, put back in the oven and cook for another 5 minutes. Remove the tin from the oven, set aside for 10 minutes, then cut along the lines you've marked again. Remove the shortbread squares carefully with a palate knife and lay on a wire rack to finish cooling. Store in an airtight tin.

75 g unrefined caster sugar, plus extra for sprinkling

175 g butter, softened

¼–½ teaspoon concentrated lavender essence or 1 tablespoon finely chopped dried lavender flowers

175 g plain flour

75 g cornflour, ground rice or fine semolina

a 27 x 18 cm, shallow, rectangular baking tin

Makes 18 shortbreads

a seafood lunch

menu for 6

Even if you're not by the coast, it's great to host a seafood lunch, especially for
health-conscious friends who like lighter food. Fish is such a popular option these days.
Wine lovers will also appreciate the chance to share a special botle of white wine,
which this simple elegant menu will show off quite perfectly. Then, having been
virtuous, everyone will fall on the gorgeous creamy dessert, a lovely summer spin on
the classic Italian tiramisù.

little seafood jellies with white wine and dill

TO DRINK A fine, minerally unoaked white such as Chablis, Sancerre, Pouilly Fumé or
a Spanish Albariño, which won't overwhelm the delicate flavours and texture of the jellies.

Sicilian-spiced seabass with grilled tomatoes
and baby fennel

TO DRINK Carry on drinking the same wine as with the first course or pick up on the Sicilian
theme with a modern Sicilian white.

strawberry tiramisù

TO DRINK This will pair beautifully with a well-chilled glass of Moscato d'Asti or
demi-sec sparkling wine.

little seafood jellies with white wine and dill

These delectable little jellies take a bit of time to assemble, but you can make them well ahead and they look really fabulous.

200 ml light dry white wine, such as Frascati

1½ tablespoons Thai fish sauce

6 sheets of leaf gelatine (or enough to set 600 ml of liquid)

200 g fresh 'queen' (small) scallops, halved

200 g cooked shelled prawns, thawed if frozen

freshly squeezed juice of 1 lemon and 1 lime, strained

90 g smoked salmon, cut into thin strips

4–5 sprigs of dill, broken into smaller sprigs

white pepper

6 glasses or glass dishes, chilled in the fridge

Serves 6

Pour the white wine into a saucepan, bring to the boil and reduce by half. Pour into a measuring jug, add the fish sauce and any liquid from the prawns, then top up with cold water up to the 600 ml mark. Lay the gelatine in a shallow dish and sprinkle over 3 tablespoons cold water. Pour the white wine mixture back into the saucepan and bring to the boil. Turn the heat right down, add the scallops and poach for 2 minutes. Remove the scallops with a slotted spoon and set aside to cool. Add the soaked gelatine to the poaching liquid and stir until thoroughly dissolved. Strain the mixture into a bowl, then place that bowl in a larger bowl of iced water to cool quickly.

Meanwhile, marinate the cooled scallops and prawns in the lemon and lime juice with a little white pepper. Once the stock has cooled down, start assembling the jellies. Drain the prawns and scallops from their marinade. Place a few prawns, scallops and pieces of smoked salmon in the bottom of each chilled glass, sprinkle over a couple of sprigs of dill then spoon over 2–3 tablespoons of the cooled stock. Place the glasses carefully in the fridge for the jelly to set (about 45 minutes), then repeat with the next layer and the next until all the seafood and dill is used up. (Try and mix up the ingredients, so you get a multicoloured effect and make sure the final layer is completely covered with stock.) The jellies should be ready to eat within an hour or 2 of making them, but you can make them to eat the next day. Serve with fine crispbreads or thinly cut slices of light rye bread and unsalted butter.

Sicilian-spiced seabass with grilled tomatoes and baby fennel

A simple dish that you can cook at the tableside if you're eating outdoors.

Soak the skewers in water for half an hour before you start. Heat a gas barbecue or light a charcoal barbecue.

Crush the fennel seeds, oregano, cumin seeds, salt, peppercorns and chilli together thoroughly in a mortar with a pestle. Make 3 slashes in each side of the fish with a sharp knife. Spray the fish with olive oil and rub the pounded spices over the fish and into the slits. Cut 2 of the lemons in half vertically, then cut 1½ into thin slices. Cut or tear the bay leaves into halves or thirds. Place half a slice of lemon and a piece of bay leaf in each slit. Cut each fennel bulb in quarters lengthways and thread the cherry tomatoes onto the skewers. Spray the fish, fennel and tomatoes with oil and grill over medium heat until charred, turning them halfway through, removing them as they are cooked. Serve with wedges of lemon.

* If whole fish don't appeal, you could make this recipe with tuna or swordfish steaks.

Conventional cooking: You could cook the fish under a conventional grill or, in the case of tuna or swordfish, in a non-stick frying pan.

1 rounded teaspoon fennel seeds

1 rounded teaspoon dried oregano

1 teaspoon cumin seeds

1 teaspoon sea salt crystals

1 teaspoon green or black peppercorns

¼ teaspoon crushed chillies

6 small seabass, gutted and scaled (ask the fishmonger or assistant at the fish counter to do this for you)*

extra virgin olive oil spray

3 unwaxed lemons

a few bay leaves

4 baby fennel bulbs

350 g cherry tomatoes

wedges of lemon, to serve

6 wooden kebab skewers

Serves 6

strawberry tiramisù

This is a slight adaptation of a fantastic recipe from Italian cookery writer Valentina Harris, which I first tasted on one of her cookery courses in Tuscany.

400 g fresh ripe strawberries
5 hard amaretti biscuits
2 large eggs, separated
40 g unrefined caster sugar
¼ teaspoon vanilla extract
4 tablespoons white rum
250 g mascarpone cheese, at room temperature
3 tablespoons whipping cream
100 ml pressed apple juice
½ 200-g pack savoiardi (sponge finger biscuits)

a medium–large, deep, glass dessert bowl

Serves 6

Hull the strawberries. Weigh out 100 g and chop them finely. Slice the remaining strawberries and set aside. Put the amaretti biscuits in a plastic bag, seal, then hit them with a rolling pin until they are the consistency of coarse breadcrumbs.

Beat the egg yolks in a bowl with an electric hand-held whisk or a whisk until pale yellow and fluffy, gradually adding the sugar as you go. Add the vanilla extract and a tablespoon of the white rum. Tip the mascarpone cheese into a large bowl, beat with a wooden spoon to soften, then gradually add the egg yolk mixture and beat until smooth. In another bowl, whisk the egg whites until they just hold a soft peak. Fold the chopped strawberries into the mascarpone cheese mixture, then carefully fold in the egg whites.

Whip the whipping cream to a similar consistency then fold that in too, together with a third of the crushed amaretti biscuits. Mix the remaining rum with the apple juice. Dip some of the savoiardi in the apple-rum mixture and lay across the base of your bowl. Reserving some sliced strawberries for decoration, arrange a layer of strawberries over the biscuits, then cover with a layer of mascarpone cream. Repeat with 1 or 2 more layers of soaked biscuits, strawberries and mascarpone cream, finishing with the mascarpone cream. Cover the bowl tightly with clingfilm and chill in the fridge for at least 5 hours.

About 1 hour before you serve up, sprinkle the remaining amaretti biscuits over the top of the tiramisù, then decorate with the remaining strawberries. Return the tiramisù to the fridge until you are ready to serve it.

an around-the-world barbecue

menu for 8

Give your barbecue a glamorous globetrotting theme with this menu, which roams from South America to the eastern Mediterranean. I've suggested a couple of delicious jug drinks as an alternative to wine, as a touch of sweetness really helps with chargrilled flavours. To refresh your palate at the end of the meal, go for the delicious and pretty sparkling wine jellies.

❧

gazpacho shots
pork and olive and cheese empanadas

TO DRINK A zesty Chilean Sauvignon Blanc or Spanish Rueda will pair well with both these dishes.

butterflied leg of lamb with cumin, lemon and garlic
kisir

TO DRINK A fruity, medium-bodied red such as a Merlot or Shiraz (you don't want too full-bodied a red with spicy or chargrilled foods). Alternatively, serve one of the two jug drinks below.

sparkling Shiraz and summer berry jellies
sparkling peach and blueberry jellies

exotic Sea Breeze
watermelon and strawberry cooler

pork and olive empanadas

Empanadas are like mini-pasties – in fact they're believed to have been introduced to Mexico by the Cornish tin miners who came to work in the tin and silver mines.

3 tablespoons light olive oil

454 g minced pork

1 onion, finely chopped

1 garlic clove, finely chopped

2 tablespoons tomato purée

½ rounded teaspoon mixed spice

125 ml passata

1 tablespoon cider vinegar

10 large pitted green olives marinated in garlic and herbs, finely chopped

2 tablespoons finely chopped parsley

sea salt and freshly ground black pepper

500 g ready-made puff pastry

1 large egg, beaten

*2 large baking trays, greased
a 9-cm pastry cutter*

Serves 8

Heat 1 tablespoon of the olive oil in a large frying pan and brown the mince. Remove to a bowl with a slotted spoon and pour off any remaining fat and meat juices. Add the remaining 2 tablespoons oil to the pan and fry the chopped onion for about 6–7 minutes until beginning to brown. Add the chopped garlic, fry for a few seconds, then return the meat to the pan. Add the tomato purée, stir in thoroughly and cook for a minute, then add the mixed spice, passata and cider vinegar. Bring to the boil and simmer for 10–15 minutes until the excess liquid has been absorbed.

Stir in the chopped olives and parsley and season to taste with salt and pepper. Set aside until cool (about 1 hour). Roll out the pastry on a floured board or work surface. Cut out rounds with the pastry cutter and place a teaspoonful of the pork filling in the centre of each one. Dampen the edges with water, fold over and press the edges together. Repeat until you have used up all the pastry and filling, re-rolling the pastry as necessary. At this point you can refrigerate or freeze the empanadas until you are ready to cook them.

To cook, preheat the oven to 225°C (425°F) Gas 7. Cut a small slit in each empanada with a sharp knife. Brush with beaten egg and place on the baking trays. Bake in the preheated oven for 8–10 minutes until puffed up and golden (slightly longer if cooking them from frozen). Serve warm.

Time-saving tip: you could serve shop-bought Mexican-style dips, such as Salsa Fresca and Guacamole.

cheese empanadas

1 garlic clove, roughly chopped

½ teaspoon salt

227 g curd cheese

¼ teaspoon sweet (dulce) pimentón or paprika

2 heaped tablespoons finely chopped shallot

2 heaped tablespoons finely chopped parsley

salt and freshly ground black pepper

Serves 8

Put the garlic in a mortar with the salt and pound with a pestle until you have a paste. Tip into the curd cheese along with the pimentón, shallot and parsley and mix thoroughly. Season with salt and pepper. Take teaspoonfuls of the mixture and use to fill the empañadas, as described on the left.

gazpacho shots

This wonderfully refreshing summer soup makes a perfect start to a barbecue. You could also serve it in small bowls with its usual garnish of finely chopped tomato, onion, cucumber and red pepper and a few crispy croûtons if you prefer to eat it that way.

¼–½ mild Spanish onion (about 90 g), roughly chopped

1 red pepper, deseeded and quartered

½ cucumber, peeled, deseeded and chopped

450 g fresh tomatoes, skinned and chopped

400-g can best-quality Italian tomatoes

1 garlic clove, crushed with ½ teaspoon salt or 1 teaspoon fresh garlic paste

3 tablespoons red wine vinegar

2 tablespoons extra virgin olive oil

a few sprigs of basil

salt, freshly ground black pepper, lemon juice and hot pepper sauce, (such as Tabasco), to taste

cucumber batons and very finely diced red pepper, to garnish

Makes 16 shot glasses

Put the chopped onion in a food processor, together with three-quarters of the pepper, roughly chopped, and the cucumber and whizz until smooth. Add the fresh tomatoes, whizz again and then add the canned tomatoes, the garlic paste, vinegar and olive oil and whizz again. Transfer to a bowl, add the basil, and refrigerate for a couple of hours. Remove the basil and pass the soup through a fine nylon sieve, pressing it well to extract all the liquid. Return to the fridge until ready to serve. Add enough iced water to make a drinkable consistency, then check the seasoning, adding salt and pepper to taste, a little vinegar or a squeeze of lemon and a dash of hot pepper sauce if you like. Serve in shot glasses with a sprinkle of tiny cubes of red pepper and a cucumber baton as a swizzle stick.

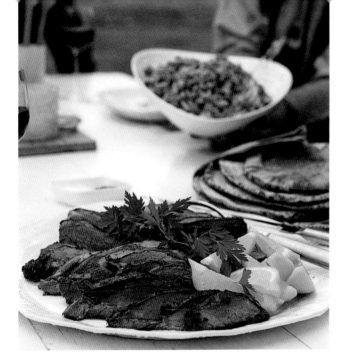

kisir

This Turkish recipe is the perfect party salad. You can vary it depending on what you have available, substituting walnuts for hazelnuts or pistachios, for example, adding some olives or some finely snipped dried apricots or replacing the dill with fresh coriander.

250 g bulghur wheat

50 g roasted hazelnuts, chopped

50 g pistachio nuts, chopped

5–6 spring onions, trimmed and thinly sliced

1/2 cucumber, peeled, deseeded and finely chopped

1 red ramiro pepper, halved, deseeded and finely chopped

3 ripe tomatoes, skinned and finely chopped

1 pomegranate

freshly squeezed juice of 2 lemons

1/2 teaspoon salt

1 teaspoon ground cumin

1 teaspoon chilli flakes

3 tablespoons extra virgin olive oil

1 tablespoon pomegranate syrup or 2 teaspoons balsamic vinegar with 1 teaspoon sugar

5 tablespoons finely chopped parsley

3 tablespoons finely chopped mint leaves

3 tablespoon finely chopped dill

sea salt and freshly ground black pepper

Serves 8

Put the bulghur wheat in a large heatproof bowl and pour over enough boiling water to just cover the grain. Leave for 15 minutes for the liquid to absorb, then pour over plenty of cold water, swirl the grain around and tip into a sieve. Squeeze the grain with your hands to extract any excess water and return the grain to the bowl.

Add the nuts, spring onions, and cucumber, pepper and tomatoes (including the seeds and pulp). Halve the pomegranate and scoop out the seeds, reserving the juice and discarding the pith. Add the pomegranate seeds to the salad.

Whisk the lemon juice and reserved pomegranate juice with the salt, cumin and chilli flakes, whisk in the olive oil and pomegranate syrup and season with salt and pepper. Tip into the salad and mix well.

Finally, mix in the chopped herbs. Toss well together and check the seasoning, adding more salt, pepper or lemon juice to taste. Cover and set aside for at least an hour before serving for the flavours to infuse.

Beers for a barbecue:

Ice-cold lager is the standard fare for barbecues, but a blonde ale or amber lager makes much more rewarding drinking.

butterflied leg of lamb with cumin, lemon and garlic

A butterflied leg of lamb – one where the bone is removed and the meat opened up to create a huge flat piece of meat – is one of the tastiest, simplest and most impressive dishes to barbecue. Order it in advance from a butcher and he'll do all the hard work for you. Serve with kisir, a mixed green salad and some flatbreads.

2 large garlic cloves, chopped

1 teaspoon coarse sea salt

1 tablespoon cumin seeds

1 teaspoon coriander seeds

1 teaspoon Herbes de Provence

1/2 teaspoon black peppercorns

1/4 teaspoon crushed chillies

freshly squeezed juice of 1 lemon

3 tablespoons olive oil

1 large butterflied leg of lamb (about 2–2.5 kg)

a large roasting tin

Serves 8

Put the garlic, salt, cumin seeds, coriander seeds, Herbes de Provence, black peppercorns and chillies in a mortar and pound with a pestle until the garlic breaks down and you have a thick paste. Gradually work in the lemon juice and oil. Work over the meat with a small, sharp knife, cutting away any excess fat, then cut the meat into 2 or 3 manageable pieces. Put the meat in a roasting tin, rub in the marinade, cover and leave in a cool place for at least 2 hours. Heat a gas barbecue to the maximum setting or light a charcoal barbecue and cook for 15–20 minutes, depending on the thickness of the meat and your preference, turning it halfway through the cooking time. Remove to a warmed carving plate, cover with foil and let rest for 15 minutes before slicing thinly.

sparkling Shiraz and summer berry jellies

9 sheets of gelatine (or enough to set 750 ml of liquid)

750 ml sparkling Shiraz or other sparkling red wine

600 g mixed fresh red berries, such as strawberries, raspberries, blackberries, blueberries, blackcurrants or redcurrants

2–3 tablespoons caster sugar, depending on how ripe your berries are

6–8 tablespoons homemade sugar syrup* or shop-bought gomme

8 glasses or small glass serving dishes

Serves 8

Put the gelatine in a flat dish and sprinkle over 4 tablespoons cold water. Leave to soak for 3 minutes until soft. Heat the wine in a microwave or saucepan until hot but not boiling. Tip the gelatine into the wine and stir to dissolve, then set aside to cool. Rinse the berries, cut the strawberries into halves or quarters, then put them in a shallow bowl, sprinkle over the sugar and leave them to macerate. Check the liquid jelly for sweetness, adding sugar syrup to taste.

Put an assortment of berries in the glasses, then pour over enough jelly to cover them. Put in the fridge to chill. As soon as the jelly has set (about 1 hour) add the rest of the fruit and jelly. Return the jellies to the fridge to set for another 45 minutes–1 hour before serving.

* To make the sugar syrup dissolve 125 g sugar in 150 ml water. Heat gently together in a pan. When all the grains are dissolved, bring to the boil and simmer for 2–3 minutes. Use it immediately or cool and store it for up to two weeks in the fridge.

sparkling nectarine and blueberry jellies

9 sheets of gelatine (or enough to set 750 ml of liquid)

750 ml sparkling peach-flavoured wine

3 ripe nectarines

2 tablespoons freshly squeezed lemon juice

200 g fresh blueberries, rinsed

8 glasses or small glass serving dishes

Serves 8–10

Put the gelatine in a flat dish and sprinkle over 4 tablespoons cold water. Leave to soak for 3 minutes until soft. Heat the wine in a microwave or saucepan until hot but not boiling. Tip the gelatine into the wine and stir to dissolve, then set aside to cool. Cut the nectarines into cubes and sprinkle with the lemon juice. Put a few blueberries and cubes of nectarine in the bottom of each glass then pour over jelly to cover. Put in the fridge to chill. As soon as the jelly has set, add the remaining fruit and jelly. Return to the fridge to set for another 45 minutes–1 hour before serving.

exotic Sea Breeze

A variation on the classic cocktail.

200 ml vodka
400 ml pomegranate juice
300 ml ruby grapefruit juice
100 ml freshly squeezed lime juice (from 2–3 limes)
2–3 teaspoons pomegranate syrup
1 pomegranate, halved and sliced
a few sprigs of fresh mint
ice cubes, to serve

Makes 6–8 glasses

Pour the vodka, pomegranate juice, ruby grapefruit juice and lime juice into a large jugful of ice. Sweeten to taste with pomegranate syrup. Garnish with pomegranate seeds and sprigs of mint to serve.

watermelon and strawberry cooler

You can't really make this unless you have a juicer, but otherwise it's one of the easiest and most refreshing summer drinks.

1 large watermelon
500 g fresh strawberries, hulled, plus extra to garnish
1 unwaxed lemon, peeled and chopped
100 ml vodka (optional)
3 sprigs of mint, leaves roughly torn
ice cubes, to serve

Makes 6–8 glasses

Cut the watermelon in half, then cut off a thin slice for garnishing. Scoop out the pulp and cut into rough chunks. Feed the watermelon, strawberries and lemon chunks through the juicer alternately. Put ice cubes into a jug (plus the vodka, if using). Pour over the juice. Add the mint and stir well. Pour into highball glasses and decorate with a wedge of watermelon and a few slices of strawberry to serve.

a family Sunday lunch

menu for 6

When several generations are involved, it's always better to play safe with the menu and stick to tried and trusted favourites like roast chicken and fruit crumbles that even small children will enjoy. And not to make the menu too long or complicated – just two courses in this case. The good news though is that these simple dishes are a great foil for fine wines – which gives the adults a treat!

~

homemade cheese nibbles

Parmesan and pistachio biscuits

Cheddar crispies

TO DRINK There's a fantastic affinity between warm cheesy biscuits and Champagne or Champagne-style sparkling wines, so that would be a great way to kick off this meal.

superlative roast chicken with sausage meatballs

crunchy roast potatoes and buttery peas

TO DRINK Drink any light- or medium-bodied red wine – a red Burgundy or other Pinot Noir or a Merlot-based red such as St. Emilion would be my top choices.

raspberry, apple and almond crumble

TO DRINK Serve a light, lemony Sauternes or Sauternes-style dessert wine such as Monbazillac or Saussignac or a late-harvest Sauvignon or Semillon.

homemade cheese nibbles

It's easy enough to buy in nibbles to have with a pre-lunch drink, but it's so simple to make your own. It can also be a fun thing to do with any budding young cooks in the family. These can be made ahead and then reheated.

Parmesan and pistachio biscuits

90 g plain flour

50 g butter, softened

50 g finely grated mature Parmesan cheese, plus extra for topping

25 g finely chopped pistachio nuts

1 large egg yolk

½ teaspoon fine sea salt

cayenne pepper, to taste

a 7-cm biscuit cutter
a baking tray, lightly greased

Makes about 18–20 biscuits

Preheat the oven to 190°C (375°F) Gas 5. Put the flour, butter, Parmesan, nuts and seasoning in a food processor and pulse until you have a crumbly mixture. Add the egg yolk and enough water (a teaspoon or two) to form a stiff dough. Transfer the dough to a lightly floured work surface or board, knead lightly and roll out quite thinly. Stamp out rounds with the biscuit cutter and carefully transfer them with a palate knife to the baking tray. Re-roll the offcuts and stamp as many more biscuits as you can get out of the dough. Sprinkle the biscuits lightly with Parmesan and bake in the preheated oven for about 15–20 minutes, until lightly browned. Leave on the baking tray for a few minutes then transfer to a wire rack to cool for 10–15 minutes. If not eating straight away, store in an airtight tin then reheat at 160°C (325°F) Gas 3 for 7–8 minutes before serving.

Cheddar crispies

110 g plain flour
½ teaspoon salt
110 g butter, chilled and cut into small cubes
110 g mature Cheddar cheese, grated
25 g crisped rice cereal
sesame seeds and poppy seeds, to garnish
freshly ground black pepper

2 baking trays, lightly greased

Makes about 20 crispies

Preheat the oven to 180°C (350°F) Gas 4.
Put the flour and salt in a bowl and season
with pepper. Add the cubed butter and rub

in until the mixture resembles coarse
breadcrumbs. Add the grated cheese and
crisped rice and pull the mixture together.
Take spoonfuls of the mixture and roll them
into small, walnut-sized balls. Arrange on
the baking trays and flatten each ball lightly
with the prongs of a fork. Sprinkle half the
crispies with sesame seeds and half with
poppy seeds and bake for 15–20 minutes
until lightly browned. Leave on the baking
trays for a few minutes, then transfer to a
wire rack to cool for 10–15 minutes. If not
eating straight away, store in an airtight tin,
then reheat at 160°C (325°F) Gas 3 for 7–8
minutes before serving.

superlative roast chicken with sausage meatballs

Everyone has their own favourite roast chicken recipe, but this is the one I go back to most often. I like to cook two small birds rather than one big one so that everyone has a chance to have their favourite bit. You can make a more sophisticated unthickened wine-based gravy if you prefer, but this is the type of gravy children (and grandparents) tend to go for!

2 small–medium chickens (about 1.25–1.35 kg), preferably organic
1 large unwaxed lemon
2 garlic cloves, unpeeled and flattened
2 small handfuls of parsley
1 tablespoon olive oil
25 g butter
sea salt and freshly ground black pepper

For the meatballs:
450 g best-quality traditional pork sausages
2 tablespoons finely chopped parsley
a little plain flour for rolling

For the gravy:
2 tablespoons plain flour
400 ml fresh chicken stock or made from 1 organic stock cube

a large roasting tin

Serves 6

Preheat the oven to 200°C (400°F) Gas 6. Grate a little zest from the lemon and reserve it for the sausage meatballs. Remove any giblets from inside the birds and stuff each of them with half a lemon, a flattened garlic clove and a small handful of parsley. Heat the olive oil gently in a small saucepan, add the butter, then when it has melted brush the chickens with the oil and butter mixture. Season the birds with salt and pepper and place them in the roasting tin, breast-side upwards. Put in the preheated oven to roast for 20 minutes until the breast begins to brown. Turn the chickens on one side and roast for a further 15 minutes, while you make the sausage meatballs (these will be added to the tin and cooked with the chicken).

Slit the skins of the sausages and tip the meat into a bowl. Add the chopped parsley, lemon zest and pepper and mix well. Form into about 18 small walnut-sized balls and brown lightly on all sides in a frying pan. Carefully pour or spoon out most of the fat and juices that have accumulated in the roasting tin and reserve them. Turn the chickens onto their other side. Add the lightly browned meatballs and cook for another 15 minutes. Finally, turn the chickens breast-side

upwards again, turn the meatballs, baste the chickens with the remaining pan juices and cook for a final 10–15 minutes until the chickens are crisp and brown and fully cooked. Take the chickens and meatballs out of the oven and transfer to a warmed serving plate. Lightly cover with foil.

To make the gravy, skim the fat off the reserved juices. Pour off all except 3 tablespoons of fat from the tin, stir in the flour and cook for a minute. Add the skimmed pan juices and a third of the stock and bring to the boil, stirring and scraping off any dark sticky bits from the side of the tin. Add the remaining stock, then simmer until thick (about 3–4 minutes). Check the seasoning, adding salt and pepper to taste, and strain the gravy into a warmed jug.

Carve the chicken and serve with the meatballs, roast potatoes and buttery peas or other child-friendly vegetables.

crunchy roast potatoes

1.5 kg roasting potatoes
5–6 tablespoons rapeseed or vegetable oil
sea salt

a medium roasting tin

Serves 6

Preheat the oven to 200°C (400°F) Gas 6. Peel the potatoes, halve or quarter them depending how big they are and place them in a large saucepan. Cover with cold water and bring to the boil. Add a little salt, boil for 5 minutes, then drain the potatoes. Pour the oil into a roasting tin and tip in the potatoes, turning them in the oil. Roast the potatoes in the preheated oven for 45 minutes, turning them halfway through the cooking time. Turn the heat up to 220°C (425°F) Gas 7 and continue to cook until the potatoes are crisp (about another 15–20 minutes).

buttery peas

450 g fresh shelled or frozen peas
a sprig of mint
40 g butter, softened
2 tablespoons finely chopped parsley or chives (optional)

Serves 6

Put the peas in a saucepan, add the mint and cover with boiling water. Bring back to the boil and cook for about 3–5 minutes until the peas are tender. Drain, add the butter and herbs, if using, and toss together well. Serve immediately.

raspberry, apple and almond crumble

The addition of raspberries to this otherwise traditional crumble not only gives it a gorgeous colour but creates a pleasing tartness that makes it a brilliant match with a fine dessert wine.

3 large Bramley apples, peeled, quartered, cored and sliced
3–4 tablespoons unrefined caster sugar
250 g fresh or frozen raspberries

For the crumble topping:
150 g plain flour
25 g ground almonds
110 g butter, chilled and cut into cubes
50 g unrefined caster sugar
25 g flaked almonds (optional)
vanilla ice cream and/or pouring cream, to serve

a shallow ovenproof dish, lightly greased

Serves 6

Put the apples in a large saucepan. Sprinkle over 3 tablespoons sugar and add 3 tablespoons water. Cover the pan, place over low heat and cook for about 15 minutes, shaking the pan occasionally until the apple pieces are soft but still holding their shape. Stir in the raspberries and check for sweetness, adding a little extra sugar if it seems too sharp. Transfer to the prepared dish and let cool.

To make the topping, put the flour and ground almonds in a large bowl. Keep cutting the butter cubes into the flour mixture until you can't get the pieces of butter any smaller, then rub the butter and flour mixture together with your fingertips, until the mixture resembles coarse breadcrumbs. Stir in the sugar and carry on rubbing for another minute. Stir in the flaked almonds, if using.

When the fruit has cooled, set the oven to 200°C (400°F) Gas 6. Spread the crumble mixture evenly over the fruit, making sure you cover the whole surface, then bake for about 35–40 minutes until the topping is golden and the fruit juices bubbling around the sides of the dish. Leave to cool for 10–15 minutes before serving.

a summer berry tea

menu for 12

A gorgeous, girly summer tea that's perfect for a celebration: a birthday, a christening or naming day or just a special treat for your mum. There are plenty of homemade treats if you fancy a bake-in or make a couple of the recipes like the meringues and the cupcakes and buy the rest in. Makes you wonder why we don't have tea more often...

mini choux puffs with crab and coriander

strawberry and mascarpone tartlets

rose petal cupcakes

pink cava and strawberry jellies

raspberry and brown sugar meringues

old-fashioned white wine cup

TO DRINK There are plenty of delicious drinks to serve if you want to stick to pink – rosé Champagne (or sparkling Zinfandel if you want a wine with a touch more sweetness) and pink lemonade would be two good choices. Or Kir Royales made with a splash of raspberry-flavoured liqueur and topped up with chilled sparkling wine.

mini choux puffs with crab and coriander

50 g butter, cut into cubes

75 g strong white flour, sifted with ¼ teaspoon fine sea salt

2 eggs, lightly beaten

2 dressed crabs

2 heaped tablespoons finely chopped fresh coriander

2 heaped tablespoons mayonnaise

2 teaspoons finely chopped pickled ginger

1 tablespoon freshly squeezed lemon juice

a little grated lemon zest

sea salt and freshly ground black pepper

2 large baking trays, lightly greased

Makes 24 puffs

Preheat the oven to 220°C (425°F) Gas 7. To make the choux puffs, melt the butter in 150 ml water in a saucepan and bring to the boil. Take off the heat, add the flour all at once and beat with a wooden spoon until the dough comes away from the side of the pan. Leave to cool for 5 minutes, then gradually beat in the eggs until you have a stiff, glossy mixture. Rinse the baking trays with cold water, shaking off any excess so they are slightly damp (this helps the pastry rise). Using 2 teaspoons spoon small blobs of the mixture onto the trays, then place in the preheated oven and cook for about 18–20 minutes until brown and well risen. Remove from the oven and cut a small slit in the base of each puff so that they don't collapse. Let cool on a wire rack.

Meanwhile, place the crab in a bowl, taking care that you don't include any pieces of shell. Add the other ingredients and mix together lightly (you don't want to pound it into a paste). Check the seasoning adding extra lemon juice or lemon zest and salt and pepper to taste.

When the choux puffs are cold, cut them in half with a serrated knife and fill with the crab mixture. Serve immediately.

strawberry and mascarpone tartlets

350 g plain flour

3 tablespoons icing sugar

175 g butter, chilled and cut into cubes

1 large egg yolk

a pinch of salt

250 g mascarpone cheese

2 tablespoons caster sugar

½ teaspoon vanilla extract

1–2 tablespoons whipping cream

375 g fresh strawberries, hulled and cut into 3

2 heaped tablespoons redcurrant jelly

a 7.5-cm pastry cutter
2 x 12-hole shallow tartlet tins

Makes 24 tartlets

To make the pastry, sift the flour and icing sugar into a large bowl. Cut the butter into the flour, then rub lightly between your fingertips until the mixture resembles coarse breadcrumbs. Mix the egg yolk with 3 tablespoons ice-cold water, add to the bowl, mix lightly and pull together into a ball, adding extra water if needed. Shape into a flat disc, put it in a plastic bag and refrigerate for at least half an hour. Roll out the pastry quite thinly and stamp out rounds, re-rolling the offcuts. Gently press the rounds into the hollows in the tartlet tins. Prick the bases and chill for another half an hour. Preheat the oven to 190°C (375°F) Gas 5. Bake the pastry cases for about 15–20 minutes until lightly coloured, then set aside and cool. Tip the mascarpone into a bowl, add the caster sugar, vanilla extract and a tablespoon of cream and beat until smooth. Add enough extra cream to give a firm but spoonable consistency. Put a heaped teaspoonful of mixture into each pastry case and top with 3 strawberry pieces, arranging them so that the pointed ends meet at the top. Melt the redcurrant jelly and brush it over the strawberries. You can chill the tarts briefly, but serve within 2 hours of making them.

rose petal cupcakes

250 g butter, softened

250 g caster sugar

4 large eggs, beaten with 1½ teaspoons vanilla extract

250 g self-raising flour, sifted twice

125 ml whole milk

For the icing:

50 g butter, softened

a few drops of pink food colouring

200 g icing sugar, sifted twice

¼ teaspoon rosewater

a small pinch of salt

2–3 tablespoons whole milk

sugar roses or other cake decorations

2 x 12-hole muffin or cake tins
approximately 24 paper cakes cases

Makes 24 cakes

Preheat the oven to 180°C (350°F) Gas 4. Tip the butter into a large bowl and beat with an electric hand-held whisk until smooth. Add the sugar about a third at a time and continue to beat until pale yellow and fluffy. Gradually add the beaten eggs and vanilla extract, adding a spoonful of flour with the last few additions. Fold in the remaining flour alternately with the milk, taking care not to overmix. Spoon into the paper cases and bake for about 20–25 minutes until well risen and firm to the touch. Remove the tins from the oven for 5 minutes then transfer the cakes to a wire rack to cool. Rinse and dry the beaters, then make the icing.

Beat the butter until soft. Pour a few drops of pink food colouring onto a teaspoon (easier to control than pouring straight from the bottle), then carefully add to the butter, pouring back any excess into the bottle. Gradually add the sifted icing sugar 2–3 tablespoonfuls at a time. Add the rosewater, salt and enough milk to make a spreadable consistency. Spread on the tops of the cupcakes and decorate with the sugar roses. Leave for 2 hours before serving.

pink cava and strawberry jellies

12 sheets of gelatine (or enough to set 1.1 litres of liquid)

1.1 litres Cava Rosado or other sparkling rosé

800 g fresh strawberries

2–3 tablespoons caster sugar, depending on how ripe your strawberries are

90–125 ml homemade sugar syrup (see page 48) or shop-bought gomme

cream or vanilla ice cream, to serve

12 wine glasses or small glass serving dishes

Serves 12

Lay the gelatine in a large flat dish and sprinkle over 5–6 tablespoons cold water. Leave to soak for 3 minutes until soft. Heat the wine in a microwave or saucepan until hot but not boiling. Tip the soaked gelatine into the wine and stir to dissolve, then set aside to cool.

Rinse the strawberries, cut them into halves or quarters to give even-sized pieces and put them into a shallow bowl, sprinkle over the sugar and leave them to macerate. Check the liquid jelly for sweetness, adding the sugar syrup to taste. Divide half the strawberries between 12 glasses or glass dishes then pour over enough jelly to cover them. Put in the fridge to chill. As soon as the jelly has set (about an hour), add the rest of the fruit and jelly. Return to the fridge to set for another 45 minutes–1 hour before serving with cream or ice cream.

* Adding a dash of strawberry-flavoured syrup or liqueur to the liquid jelly will make this even more delicious.

raspberry and brown sugar meringues

I love the little explosions of fruit in the middle of these meringues. They won't keep as long as conventional meringues, so do eat them within two to three hours of making them.

4 large egg whites, at room temperature

150 g unrefined caster sugar

50 g light brown muscovado sugar, sifted

200 g frozen raspberries, unthawed

2 large, non-stick baking trays, lightly greased with flavourless oil or lined with baking parchment

Makes 16 meringues

Preheat the oven to 150°C (300°F) Gas 2. Put the egg whites in a large, clean grease-free bowl and start to whisk them (easiest with an electric hand-held whisk). Increase the speed as they begin to froth up, moving the whisk around the bowl, until they just hold a peak (about 2–3 minutes). Gradually add the caster sugar a teaspoonful at a time, beating the meringue well between each addition. When half the caster sugar has been incorporated, add the rest of the caster sugar a dessertspoonful at a time. Gradually add the brown sugar, then gently fold in the frozen raspberries, ensuring that they are fully coated by the meringue.

Using 2 dessertspoons, carefully spoon the meringues onto the prepared baking trays. Place in the preheated oven and immediately reduce the heat to 140°C (275°F) Gas 1. Bake for 1¼ hours until the meringues are firm. Turn off the heat and leave the meringues to cool in the oven.

You can refrigerate the meringues for up to 3 hours, lightly covered with clingfilm, before serving.

old-fashioned white wine cup

The great virtue of white wine cups is that you can use a really basic, inexpensive dry white wine as the base. In fact, it's a positive advantage to do so. Most modern whites have too much up-front fruit flavour and alcohol for this delicate, quintessentially English summery drink.

2 x 75-cl bottles very dry white wine, such as basic Vin Blanc or Muscadet, chilled

750 ml soda water, chilled

100–125 ml homemade sugar syrup (see page 48) or shop-bought gomme

50–100 ml brandy

about 20 ice cubes, to serve

orange, lemon, apple, kiwi, strawberry and cucumber slices, to serve

a few mint or borage leaves, to garnish

Makes 16 glasses

Mix the wine and soda in a jug and add sugar syrup and brandy to taste. Prepare the fruit and add to the mix, together with ice cubes, just before serving. Serve in wine glasses, garnished with the mint.

tea

A tea party is the perfect opportunity to serve some interesting teas and tisanes: Earl Grey or Lady Grey, for example, or fragrant Orange Pekoe. Ideally, you should make them from loose leaves in a teapot, warming the pot first and infusing them for 2–3 minutes. Encourage your guests to drink them without milk and with honey rather than sugar. Another delicious option is a tisane or infusion of fresh lemon verbena leaves (*verveine* to the French who are mad about it), which makes a really refreshing, slightly citrussy drink.

come round for a drink

great ideas for simple entertaining

The easiest way to entertain people is to invite them round for a drink. Of course, you don't just mean a drink, but a bite to eat too. In the past that might have meant a few nuts or crisps, olives and cubes of cheese, or possibly a dip with a few crisp vegetables or crackers to dunk in it. Not a great deal because the presumption would have been that there was a 'proper' meal to follow. Nowadays with both eating and entertaining being a great deal more relaxed and casual, it's more than likely that the food you serve will constitute a light meal, supplanting supper, and need to be more substantial.

Inviting friends round for a drink is more a message to your guests that this is a low-key affair without formal courses, that neither they or you has to make a special effort and that you just want the pleasure of enjoying an evening with them. It's a good way to entertain when all parties are pressed for time, not least because these days, whatever food or drink you choose to serve, you can buy virtually everything in. Whether it's Spanish tapas, Middle Eastern or Mexican dips, Indian street snacks or Japanese sushi, you can find it ready-made in your local supermarket. All you have to do is present it with a little care and style, and choose an interesting drink to accompany it.

Over the next few pages you'll find some easy ideas for theming an invitation to drinks, which you can easily adapt to larger numbers. You'll also find some ideas in other sections of the book, such as the Provençal snacks on pages 28–29 and the Chinese dim sum on pages 122–123.

sushi and sake

Serve an attractive selection of ready-made sushi with chilled sake – you could lay on a few light lagers or sparkling wine for those who don't think they like sake. If you want something sweet, you could serve some little jellies or Japanese-style cakes (which you can find in oriental supermarkets or order them from a local Japanese restaurant).

Indian street snacks

Serve a selection of shop-bought classic deep-fried snacks, such as onion bhajias, pakoras and samosas with fresh coriander chutney or raita and a choice of lighter beers (pale ales, pilseners and wheat beers would make a good selection). By all means lay on some wine – oddly, sparkling white wine works well with spicy snacks or an off-dry white such as Riesling. You could also serve jugs of mango lassi (yoghurt mixed with mango purée and water).

go Greek

Serve a selection of shop-bought mezedes such as hummus, taramasalata, stuffed vine leaves, feta cheese and marinated olives with warmed pitta bread, and one of Greece's vivid lemony white wines, such as Assyrtiko from the island of Santorini. More adventurous guests might enjoy octopus or squid with ouzo. Finish with fresh fruits or syrup-drenched pastries served with the glorious Samos Muscat dessert wine.

beer and cheese

An alternative to wine and cheese that gives you a chance to explore and enjoy some of the fantastic craft beers that are now available. Choose four to six different styles and have a tasting, followed by some good artisanal cheeses and breads. You could even serve a cheesecake with a fruit beer to finish.

Margaritas and tostaditas

Why not have a get-together with a Mexican flavour? You can serve your Margaritas Mexican-style with tortilla chips and a simple salsa but here's a slightly dressier way of serving them.

prawn and guacamole topping

For the marinade:

freshly squeezed juice of ½ a lime

1½ tablespoons olive oil

1 garlic clove, crushed

1 tablespoon finely chopped fresh coriander

200 g cooked tiger prawns

200 g shop-bought or homemade guacamole

large tortilla chips, to serve

Makes sufficient to top 12–14 large tortilla chips

Mix the ingredients for the marinade together and pour over the prawns. Cover and marinate for at least an hour. Spoon the guacamole onto tortilla chips and top with a prawn.

crab, mango and basil topping

2 rounded tablespoons mayonnaise

1 small red chilli, deseeded and finely chopped

2 spring onions, trimmed and finely chopped

a little finely grated fresh ginger (about ½ teaspoon)

1–2 tablespoons freshly squeezed lemon juice

175 g fresh white or white and brown crab meat

75 g peeled and finely diced ripe mango, plus mango shavings made using a vegetable peeler or sharp knife, to garnish

6 large basil leaves

sea salt and cayenne pepper

large tortilla chips, to serve

Makes sufficient to top 12–14 large tortilla chips

Mix the mayonnaise with the chilli, spring onions, ginger and 1 tablespoon of the lemon juice. Fold in the crab and mango. Season to taste with salt, cayenne pepper and extra lemon juice. Refrigerate. Just before serving, finely shred the basil leaves and fold into the crab mixture. Spoon onto tortilla chips and top with a mango shaving.

classic frozen Margaritas

24 ice cubes

freshly squeezed juice of 3–4 limes (about 150 ml)

1½ teaspoons unrefined caster sugar

300 ml silver tequila

150 ml Triple Sec, Cointreau or Grand Marnier

1 lime, to garnish

salt (optional)*

8 wide-rimmed Martini or Margarita glasses, rims salted (optional)

Makes 6–8 drinks

Place the ice cubes in a blender goblet with the lime juice and sugar. Whizz until it forms a frozen slush. Add the tequila and Triple Sec and whizz again. Pour into the prepared glasses and decorate with a slice of lime.

* The traditional presentation is to frost your glasses with salt. Simply run a wedge of lime round the rim and invert the glass in a saucer of sea salt.

iced strawberry Margaritas

350 g fresh strawberries

4–6 tablespoons Cointreau or Triple Sec

500-ml tub shop-bought strawberry sorbet

225 ml silver tequila

2–4 tablespoons freshly squeezed lime juice

crushed ice, to serve

3–4 wide-rimmed Martini or Margarita glasses

Makes 3–4 drinks

Hull the strawberries and reserve a few for the garnish. Slice the rest roughly, then put half in a blender with 2 tablespoons Cointreau and whizz until smooth. Tip in half the sorbet, add half the tequila and 1 tablespoon of the lime juice and whizz again. Taste, adjusting the amount of Cointreau or lime juice (or tequila!) if you think it needs it. Fill the glasses with crushed ice and put a few slices of the reserved strawberries in each. Pour over the Margarita and stir. Repeat with the remaining ingredients.

tapas and sherry

menu for 6

Although this is essentially a drinks party with snacks, you can actually offer some quite substantial food – what the Spanish would refer to as 'raciones'. As with other menus, you can buy in many of the dishes – see page 71 for my deli-bought suggestions – but there are some great recipes here that I use regularly, to add to your repertoire. As I love sherry, this is one of my favourite ways of entertaining.

albondigas

courgette, potato and onion tortilla

braised broad beans with pancetta and mint

mixed seafood salad with lemon, caper
and parsley dressing

TO DRINK A chilled fino manzanilla sherry would go well with all these savoury tapas. Alternatively, you could offer Spain's famous sparkling wine, Cava, a dry Spanish 'rosado', unoaked white Rioja or Rueda or even a Spanish beer.

Spanish-style orange and almond cake

TO DRINK Serve a sweet oloroso sherry or a sherry-based orange liqueur.

albondigas (meatballs)

I adore meatballs of any description, so this is one of my favourite tapas. They are time consuming, but children will love helping you make them – and can eat any leftovers!

3 tablespoons Spanish extra virgin olive oil

½ bunch of spring onions, trimmed and very thinly sliced or 1 small onion, very finely chopped

3 garlic cloves, crushed

400 g spicy pork sausages

500 g lean minced beef

60 g pimento-stuffed green olives, very finely chopped

2 tablespoons very finely chopped flat leaf parsley

2–3 tablespoons plain flour

4–5 tablespoons sunflower or light olive oil

½ teaspoon sweet (dulce) Spanish pimentón or paprika

500 ml passata

sea salt and freshly ground black pepper

a roasting tin or ovenproof dish cocktail sticks

Serves 8

Preheat the oven to 190°C (375°F) Gas 5. Heat a large frying pan over medium heat and add 2 tablespoons of the olive oil. Fry the spring onions and 2 garlic cloves for a couple of minutes without colouring until soft and set aside. Slit and pull away the skins of the sausages, put the sausagemeat in a large bowl with the minced beef and mix together thoroughly (hands are easiest, but you can use a fork and/or a wooden spoon). Add the softened spring onions and garlic, olives and parsley, season with salt and pepper and mix again until all the ingredients are thoroughly amalgamated.

Sprinkle some of the flour over a chopping board. Lightly flour your hands before taking heaped teaspoonfuls of the meat mixture and rolling them between your palms into small meatballs. Flour your board and hands again as necessary. Wipe the frying pan with kitchen paper and put back on the heat. Add 3 tablespoons of the oil and fry the meatballs in batches, browning them on all sides, adding extra oil if needed. Put the meatballs in the roasting tin or ovenproof dish as you finish them.

Discard any remaining oil in the pan, rinse clean and wipe with kitchen paper. Replace over the heat. Add the remaining oil, garlic and the pimentón, stir for a few seconds and tip in the passata. Cook for 2–3 minutes, then check the seasoning, adding salt and pepper to taste. Pour the sauce over the meatballs and bake in the preheated oven for 35–40 minutes until they are nicely browned, turning them in the sauce halfway through the cooking time. Serve warm on cocktail sticks.

courgette, potato and onion tortilla

Tortilla is one of those dishes that is really straightforward, but hard to make it taste as it did on your Spanish holiday. The secret is patience, as it needs a good deal more time than a conventional omelette.

7 tablespoons Spanish extra virgin olive oil

3 medium or 2 large courgettes, cut into slices about 1 cm thick

350 g salad potatoes, very thinly sliced*

1 large Spanish onion, very thinly sliced

1 rounded teaspoon finely chopped thyme (optional)

8 eggs, lightly beaten

sea salt and freshly ground black pepper

*a wok
a deep-sided, non-stick frying pan about 23–24 cm wide*

Serves 6–8

Heat a wok over medium heat, add 3 tablespoons of the olive oil and stir-fry the courgette slices until lightly browned (about 5 minutes). Remove them from the pan with a slotted spoon, leaving behind as much of the oil as possible, and set aside. Add another 3 tablespoons of oil to the pan, heat for a minute, then tip in the potato slices and stir with a spatula to ensure they are separate and well coated with oil. Fry, stirring, for about 5–6 minutes until they start to brown, then turn the heat down, cover the pan and cook for another 10–15 minutes until the potatoes are tender, turning them every so often to ensure they don't catch. Remove them from the pan, again leaving behind as much oil as possible. Add a little more oil if necessary, then add the onion and stir-fry for about 6–7 minutes until soft and beginning to brown. Add the thyme, then tip the other ingredients back into the pan, mix together lightly and season well with salt and pepper. Tip the vegetables into the beaten eggs and mix well.

Heat the smaller frying pan until moderately hot, add a little oil, wipe off the excess with kitchen paper, then pour in the egg mixture. Lift the vegetables up around the edge of the pan to allow the liquid egg to trickle down to the base until most of the egg is set, then turn the heat down a little and leave the tortilla to cook for about 5 minutes while you preheat the grill to moderate. Slip the pan under the grill about 12 cm from the heat until the egg on top of the tortilla is puffed up and lightly browned and the egg in the middle of the tortilla has set (about another 5–6 minutes). Leave the tortilla to cool in the pan, then loosen it around the edges. Put a plate over the pan and flip the tortilla over so that it lands bottom-side upwards. Cut into slices or wedges and serve at room temperature.

* As you slice the potatoes, put them in a bowl of cold water to get rid of the excess starch, then give them a good swirl, drain off the water and dry them with kitchen paper.

braised broad beans with pancetta and mint

A delicious and easy tapas that goes particularly well with the meatballs or the Spanish air-dried ham Serrano. You can obviously make this with fresh broad beans in season, but the frozen ones are excellent and cut down cooking time.

3 tablespoons extra virgin olive oil

1 onion, finely chopped

65 g cubed pancetta

1–2 large garlic cloves, crushed

½ teaspoon sweet (dulce) Spanish pimentón or ¼ teaspoon paprika

450 g frozen baby broad beans

300 ml hot vegetable stock

1 heaped tablespoon chopped flat leaf parsley

1 heaped tablespoon chopped mint leaves

sea salt and freshly ground black pepper

Serves 6–8

Heat a medium frying pan or flameproof casserole over medium heat, add 2 tablespoons of the olive oil and the onion and pancetta and fry gently for about 4–5 minutes until the onion is soft. Add the crushed garlic and pimentón, stir, then tip in the broad beans. Pour in the hot stock and bring to the boil, then cook for about 10 minutes until the beans are tender.

Take off the heat, cool for about 8–10 minutes, then add the herbs and remaining olive oil. Check the seasoning, adding salt and pepper to taste. Serve at room temperature.

mixed seafood salad with lemon, caper and parsley dressing

A mixed pack of seafood makes the basis for this easy seafood salad, which goes fabulously well with chilled manzanilla sherry.

4 tablespoons Spanish extra virgin olive oil

1 large garlic clove, crushed

500 g mixed seafood cocktail, thawed if frozen

150 g small shelled prawns, thawed if frozen

2 teaspoons finely grated lemon zest

1½–2 tablespoons freshly

squeezed lemon juice

2 tablespoons capers, rinsed and finely chopped

3 tablespoons finely chopped flat leaf parsley

sea salt and freshly ground black pepper

Serves 6

Heat a large frying pan over medium heat, add the olive oil and garlic and fry for a few seconds, then tip in the seafood cocktail and prawns. Turn the heat up and stir-fry for a couple of minutes so that the seafood heats right through.

Remove from the heat and add the grated lemon zest, lemon juice and capers and most of the parsley, saving a few leaves for garnishing. Mix together lightly and thoroughly. Check the seasoning adding salt and pepper to taste and extra lemon juice or olive oil if you think it needs it. Leave to cool, then cover and refrigerate for a few hours to allow the flavours to amalgamate.

Spanish-style orange and almond cake

This featherlight, syrup-drenched orange and almond cake, makes an impressive finale to a tapas meal.

4 large eggs, separated
1 heaped tablespoon finely grated orange zest
100 g unrefined caster sugar
125 g ground almonds, sifted
1 teaspoon orange flower water

For the syrup:
freshly squeezed juice of 1½ oranges and 1 lemon (about 125 ml juice in total)
75 g unrefined caster sugar
1 cinnamon stick

½ teaspoon orange flower water

a 21-cm cake tin, lined with a round of baking parchment

Serves 8–10

Preheat the oven to 180°C (350°F) Gas 4. Put the egg yolks in a large bowl with the orange zest and all except 1 tablespoon of the sugar and beat well, until light and moussey (about 2–3 minutes). Fold in a third of the almonds, then the next third and finally the remaining third. (The mixture will be quite thick, but don't worry!) Wash and dry the beaters thoroughly. Whisk the egg whites in a separate bowl until just stiff, then add the remaining sugar and briefly whisk again. Take a couple of spoonfuls of the meringue and fold it into the cake mixture to loosen it. Fold in half the remaining meringue then, when the mixture is quite loose, carefully fold in the final portion, taking care not to overmix. Spoon the cake mixture into the prepared tin and bake for about 40–45 minutes until the surface of the cake is well browned and firm and the cake has shrunk away from the side of the tin. Remove from the oven and cool for 5 minutes, then turn out on a wire rack.

While the cake is cooking, make the syrup. Put the orange and lemon juices in a small saucepan, add the sugar, cinnamon stick and orange flower water and heat gently, stirring occasionally, until all the grains of sugar have dissolved. Bring to the boil and boil without stirring for about 4–5 minutes. Strain and cool. After the cake has cooled for about 15 minutes, put it upside-down on a plate, pierce it in several places with a skewer and spoon over some of the syrup a tablespoonful at a time. Carefully turn the cake over, pierce the top of the cake and spoon over as much of the remaining syrup as the cake will absorb. Leave to finish cooling before serving.

* You can dress this up into a dinner party dessert by serving the cake with some sliced caramelized oranges and a spoonful of whipped, sweetened cream flavoured with a few drops of orange flower water.

deli-bought tapas

You can buy everything you need to put together a selection of Spanish-style tapas in a deli or a supermarket these days: fine slices of serrano or (even better) Pata Negra (acorn-fed ham), chorizo, thin slices of Manchego cheese, toasted and salted Marcona almonds, large caper berries, marinated olives and piquillo peppers, which taste particularly good warmed through with a little olive oil and garlic, prepared as follows:-

Warm a couple of large spoonfuls of good olive oil over low heat. Add a few very finely sliced garlic cloves and keep over low heat for about 10 minutes without allowing them to colour. Drain a jar or can of red piquillo peppers, quarter the peppers and warm them through in the garlic-infused oil. Serve with crusty bread on the side to mop up the juices.

deli-bought dessert tapas

It is equally easy to put together a Spanish-inspired 'dessert tapas' selection including turrón (Spanish nougat, which comes in a variety of versions, including hard and soft), Spanish biscuits, such as hazelnut Polvorónes or Ines Rosáles, tortas de aceite and anis (deliciously crispy aniseed and olive oil biscuits), dried fruits such as figs and large moscatel raisins, an almond cake (or make the one opposite) and maybe some Spanish chocolates. You could partner them with a sweet oloroso sherry, good coffee and Spanish brandy.

Another easy, delicious idea is to serve scoops of vanilla ice cream with ultra-rich, syrupy PX (Pedro Ximenez) sherry trickled over the top.

cooling supper for a hot evening

menu for 6

It might seem a contradiction to suggest that the ideal food to serve on a sultry evening is spicy food, but if you think about those countries that habitually have hot weather like India or Thailand, you realize that that is exactly what you need. What you will also notice is that they serve it lukewarm or cold so that the heat doesn't become overwhelming. This is an eclectic modern menu to serve to adventurous friends who love new tastes and flavours.

ginger and lemongrass Martinis

TO DRINK Kick the evening off with a fragrant Martini; cocktails are always good on a hot evening. You can make a non-alcoholic version for those who don't drink or serve one of the refreshing new green tea-based drinks.

spiced mango, carrot and chilli soup

Thai-style beef with tomato and herb salad
prawn and cucumber sesame noodles

TO DRINK With the soup and salads I suggest a dry aromatic white like an Alsace Riesling, an Austrian Grüner Veltliner or a limey Australian Verdelho. A Belgian witbier (cloudy wheat beer) would also work well.

exotic fruits with Piña Colada sherbet

spiced mango, carrot and chilli soup

An unusual and stunning-looking chilled soup that is wonderfully refreshing on a warm evening. Make sure your mango is ripe or you won't get the depth of flavour you need. You might want a slightly less ripe one for the garnish.

3 tablespoons grapeseed or vegetable oil
1 onion, roughly chopped
4 carrots, thinly sliced
½ teaspoon ground turmeric
1 teaspoon grated fresh ginger or ginger paste
500 ml vegetable stock
300 g (peeled, stoned weight) ripe mango, diced
freshly squeezed juice of 1–1½ limes (3–4 tablespoons)
sea salt and cayenne pepper

To serve:
low-fat natural yoghurt
100 g mango, peeled and cut into small dice, to serve
sweet chilli sauce
a few coriander leaves
Japanese rice crackers, to serve (optional)

Serves 4–6

Heat the oil over low heat in a large, lidded saucepan or flameproof casserole. Add the onion, stir, cover and cook gently for 5 minutes. Add the carrots, stir, replace the lid and continue to cook for another 10 minutes. Stir in the turmeric and ginger, cook for a minute then pour in the vegetable stock. Bring to the boil and simmer until the carrot is cooked – about 20 minutes. Set aside until cool (about an hour).

Strain off the liquid into a bowl and tip the vegetables into a food processor along with the mango. Add 2–3 tablespoons of the liquid and whizz until smooth. Add half the remaining liquid and whizz again. Tip the purée into the bowl with the rest of the liquid and mix well. Add 3 tablespoons of the lime juice and season with salt and cayenne pepper. Cover and refrigerate for at least 2 hours.

To serve, pour in enough chilled water to create a thin, spoonable consistency. Check the seasoning, adding extra lime juice to taste if needed. Ladle the soup into bowls and spoon over a swirl of yoghurt. Scatter with a few cubes of mango, drizzle over a little sweet chilli sauce and scatter with coriander leaves. Serve with Japanese rice crackers on the side.

Thai-style beef with tomato and herb salad

Thai cuisine features some great meat-based salads that are wonderfully zingy and refreshing. The amount of chilli you use is up to you. You can leave out the roasted chillies and only use fresh ones if you like, but I like the smoky flavour they give.

2 tablespoons Thai fragrant rice
1 teaspoon crushed chillies
1–2 thick slices of rump steak (about 900 g in total and about 2 cm thick), trimmed of any fat
1½ tablespoons sunflower or light olive oil
3–4 teaspoons unrefined caster sugar
freshly squeezed juice of 3 limes, about 7–9 tablespoons
4 tablespoons Thai fish sauce
2 large garlic cloves, grated
2–3 medium-hot fresh red chillies, deseeded and very finely chopped
8 small shallots, very thinly sliced
or a bunch of spring onions, trimmed and thinly sliced
5 heaped tablespoons coriander leaves, chopped
3 heaped tablespoons mint leaves, chopped
250 g cherry tomatoes, quartered
1 cos lettuce heart, washed and crisped in the fridge

a ridged grill pan

Serves 6–8

Heat a small frying pan over medium heat, add the rice and cook, stirring occasionally until golden and fragrant (about 5 minutes). Take off the heat, allow to cool for a couple of minutes, then grind in a mortar with a pestle or the end of a rolling pin. Toast the crushed chillies in the same way for a few seconds, add to the rice and grind again. Heat a ridged grill pan for about 3 minutes until smoking hot, rub the steak the oil and cook for about 1½ minutes each side until charred but still rare (or longer if you prefer). Set aside to cool while you make the dressing.

Dissolve the sugar in the lime juice, add the fish sauce, the garlic and half the chopped chillies and taste. Add more fish sauce and chillies if you think the dressing needs it and a little water if the dressing is too strong. Slice the steak thinly, then tip the slices together with any juices into a bowl with the dressing and add the shallots, coriander, mint and cherry tomatoes. Toss, then sprinkle with the toasted rice mixture. Finely shred the cos lettuce and arrange the shredded leaves on a large platter. Top with the dressed beef to serve.

prawn and cucumber sesame noodles

A clean, refreshing noodle salad that goes particularly well with the beef.

250 g fine rice or dried soba noodles

400 g cooked shelled prawns, thawed if frozen

⅔ cucumber, peeled, quartered, deseeded and cut into diagonal slices

½ bunch of spring onions, trimmed and thinly sliced

For the dressing:

6 tablespoons Japanese seasoned rice vinegar

2 tablespoons light soy sauce

4 tablespoons sunflower or rapeseed oil

2 tablespoons sesame oil

1½ teaspoons finely grated fresh ginger or ginger paste

1½ teaspoons finely grated garlic or garlic paste

4 tablespoons toasted sesame seeds*

5 tablespoons finely chopped coriander leaves

sea salt (optional)

Serves 6–8

Break the dried noodles into thirds and put them in a heatproof bowl. Pour over boiling water, leave for 3 minutes, then drain and rinse under cold water. Put them in a large serving bowl and add the prawns, cucumber and spring onions.

Pour the rice vinegar and soy sauce into a separate bowl, then whisk in the sunflower oil and sesame oil. Whisk in the ginger and garlic, add the dressing to the noodles and toss together. Check the seasoning, adding a little salt if necessary. Just before serving, sprinkle over the sesame seeds and chopped coriander and toss again.

*To toast the sesame seeds, warm them in a dry frying pan over low heat until they begin to change colour.

exotic fruits

Make up a large, attractive platter of exotic fruits such as pineapple, mango, papaya, passion fruit, star fruit, physalis and lychees so that your guests can help themselves.

Piña Colada sherbet

This is a cross between an ice cream and a sorbet. It makes a fantastically refreshing end to the meal. Don't make it more than a few days in advance, as it won't keep like a commercial ice cream.

150 g unrefined caster sugar

1 ripe pineapple

200 ml coconut cream

6 tablespoons freshly squeezed lime juice (2–3 limes)

4 tablespoons white rum

2 large egg whites, beaten

Serves 6–8

Put the sugar in a pan with 200 ml water over very low heat, stirring occasionally, until the sugar has dissolved. Bring to the boil without stirring and boil for about 4 minutes. Set aside to cool. Quarter the pineapple, cut away the tough central core and cut off the skin. Cut into cubes and pass through a juicer.* This should give you about 550–600 ml juice. Mix in the coconut cream, cooled sugar syrup, lime juice and rum, which should give you just over 1 litre liquid.

Cover, transfer the sherbet mixture to the fridge and chill for a couple of hours. Pour into an ice cream machine and churn, adding the egg whites halfway through. (You may need to do this in 2 batches). If you haven't got an ice cream machine, pour the sherbet mix into a lidded plastic box and freeze for about 1½ hours or until beginning to harden at the edges. Put the egg whites in a food processor, process briefly until frothy, then tip in the half-frozen sherbet mixture and whizz until smooth. Return the sherbet mix to the freezer, freeze for another hour, then whizz again. Freeze and whizz a third time for extra smoothness. Leave to harden. Before serving, remove the sherbet from the freezer and leave to mellow in the fridge for about 20 minutes. Serve with a selection of tropical fruits.

* If you haven't got a juicer, remove all the little brown 'eyes' from the pineapple, cut into cubes, purée in a food processor and strain the juice.

ginger and lemongrass Martinis

Bottled cordials make rustling up a cocktail incredibly easy. You can vary the quantities depending how gingery or how sweet you like your drinks, but this works for me.

crushed ice

1 shot ginger and lemongrass cordial

2 shots vodka

a thinly pared slice of lemon zest

a short length of lemongrass stalk, outer layer removed, to garnish

a Martini glass

Serves 1

Fill a cocktail shaker with ice. Add the cordial and vodka and shake well. Strain into a Martini glass. Holding the piece of lemon zest, twist it over the drink so the lemon oil in the zest drops on the surface then drop it into the drink. Garnish with the lemongrass.

a farmers' market supper

menu for 6

There's nothing more inspirational than a visit to the local farmers' market, especially in spring when the new season's vegetables finally arrive after the bleak stretch of winter. Invite friends round to share the bounty the same evening and enjoy the produce at its freshest and best.

pea and Parma ham crostini

farmers' market salad with goats' cheese, asparagus and roast beets

spring vegetable pasta with lemon

strawberry, rose and rhubarb fool

TO DRINK At this time of year I like to keep the drink light and white. The green sappy, citrussy flavours of Sauvignon Blanc are a perfect choice with the first two courses of this menu. I'd choose one from the Loire like a Sancerre or Pouilly Fumé. With the pasta, I'd serve a good Italian Pinot Grigio or a Chablis. You could offer non-drinkers an elderflower spritzer.

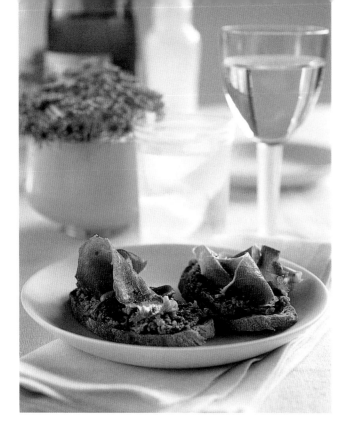

farmers' market salad with goats' cheese, asparagus and roast beets

This salad came about a couple of years ago as a result of a visit to my local farmers' market and has remained a firm favourite ever since. Don't let memories of vinegar-soused beetroot put you off – roast beetroot has a fabulously sweet, earthy flavour that just needs a few salad leaves and some fresh tangy white goats' cheese to set it off.

a bunch of fresh beetroot

4 tablespoons sunflower oil

800 g broad bean pods

a bunch of fresh asparagus

3 tablespoons rice vinegar

2 tablespoons walnut oil

100 g mixed salad leaves, such as rocket, watercress, baby spinach or mustard leaves

200 g goats' cheese

a small handful of chopped green herbs, such as parsley or dill

a few chives, snipped

sea salt and freshly ground black pepper

Serves 4–6

Preheat the oven to 200°C (400°F) Gas 6. Cut off the beetroot tops and trim off the roots. Wash the beetroot under running water to remove any dirt and dry with kitchen paper. Take a large piece of foil and place it on a baking tray. Oil it lightly, place the beetroot in the centre and scrunch the edges of the foil together to make a loose tent. Cook in the preheated oven for 50 minutes–1 hour or until tender. When cool enough to handle, peel off the skins and cut into quarters or smaller wedges.

Meanwhile, pod the broad beans and cook them in boiling water for about 8–10 minutes or until just cooked. When cool enough to handle, pop the beans out of their skins. Cut the tips of the asparagus off about a third of the way down the stalk and steam or microwave for about 3–4 minutes until just tender. Set aside and let cool.

Shake the vinegar, oils, salt and pepper together in a screw-top glass jar. Use half to lightly dress the beetroot. Divide the leaves between 4 plates and drizzle with a little of the remaining dressing. Arrange the beetroot wedges over the leaves and top with roughly torn chunks of goats' cheese and the broad beans. Scatter over the herbs, trickle over the remaining dressing and grind a little black pepper over the top. Serve with some crusty bread.

pea and Parma ham crostini

The new season's peas are so deliciously sweet that you want to enjoy them every which way you can.

250 g shelled fresh or frozen peas

2 spring onions

40 g finely grated aged pecorino or Parmesan cheese

1 tablespoon finely chopped mint or dill

2 tablespoons fruity olive oil

18 ciabatta toasts (see page 28)

125 g thinly sliced Parma ham or other air-dried ham, torn or cut in half

salt and freshly ground black pepper

freshly squeezed lemon juice, to taste

Makes 18 crostini

Cook the peas in boiling water for 2–3 minutes or until just tender. Drain under cold running water. Trim and cut the spring onions in half lengthways, then slice very thinly.

Put the peas and onions in a food processor and pulse until you get a chunky spread. Add the pecorino and mint and pulse again, then stir in the olive oil. Season to taste with salt, pepper and lemon juice. Spread the mixture thickly on ciabatta toasts and drape with a piece of ham. Serve immediately.

spring vegetable pasta with lemon

This dish is admittedly more vegetable than pasta, but it's one of the most delicious ways to enjoy the new season's produce. You can vary the vegetables depending on what's available. Baby courgettes also work well, as does fennel. The key thing is to cook them until they're only just done to preserve their delicate flavour and bright green colour.

a small bunch of asparagus
150 g shelled fresh peas
a few stalks of sprouting broccoli
150 g shelled broad beans
110 g butter
1 leek or ½ bunch of spring onions, thinly sliced
284-ml carton double cream
300 g dried egg pasta shapes, such as Campanelle
freshly squeezed juice of 2–3 lemons (about 125 ml)
3 heaped tablespoons finely chopped parsley
2 heaped tablespoons each finely chopped dill and chives
sea salt and freshly ground black pepper
freshly shaved Parmesan cheese or grana padano, to serve

Serves 6

Snap the asparagus spears two-thirds down the stalks and discard the woody ends. Cut the remaining stem into short lengths. Steam or microwave them for about 2–3 minutes until just cooked and refresh with cold water. Repeat with the other vegetables – steaming them individually until just cooked. (Pop the broad beans out of their skins for an even sweeter taste).

Gently melt the butter in a large saucepan or flameproof casserole and cook the leek for a couple of minutes until starting to soften. Tip in the other vegetables, lightly toss with the butter, cover the pan and leave over very low heat, adding the cream once the vegetables have heated through.

Cook the pasta following the instructions on the packet. Reserve a little of the cooking water and drain well. Tip the drained pasta into the vegetables and toss together. Add the lemon juice and herbs, season with salt and pepper and toss together lightly. Check the seasoning, adding extra salt, pepper, lemon juice or a little of the reserved pasta cooking water to lighten the sauce if you think it needs it. Serve in warm bowls with shavings of Parmesan.

strawberry, rose and rhubarb fool

Rhubarb and strawberries have an extraordinary affinity and fortunately come into season at the same time of year.

400 g fresh rhubarb
3 tablespoons unrefined caster sugar
225 g fresh, ripe strawberries, plus a few extra to garnish
2–3 tablespoons rose syrup or rosewater and extra caster sugar
300 g Greek yoghurt
284-ml carton whipping cream

6 glasses or glass serving dishes

Serves 6

Slice the rhubarb and put it in a saucepan with the sugar and 2 tablespoons water. Put a lid on the pan and heat over low heat until the fruit comes to the boil, then turn the heat down and simmer for 7–10 minutes until the fruit is soft. Tip the fruit into a sieve over a bowl and drain off the juice.

Hull the strawberries, put 225 g of them in a food processor and whizz until smooth. Add the drained rhubarb and 1 tablespoon rose syrup or 2 teaspoons rosewater with 1 tablespoon caster sugar and whizz again. Tip the purée into a bowl and leave to cool. Tip the yoghurt into a large bowl. In a separate bowl, whip the cream until just holding its shape and sweeten to taste with rose syrup or rosewater and sugar. Fold half the cream into the yoghurt. Fold half the puréed strawberry and rhubarb into the yoghurt and cream mixture then lightly mix the remaining cream and the rest of the rhubarb and strawberry purée to create a marbled effect.

Spoon the fool into individual glasses and chill until ready to serve. Slice the remaining strawberries and sprinkle with a few drops of rose syrup or a little sugar. Use the strawberry slices to decorate the top of each glass.

Time-saving tip: If you don't have time to make a dessert, simply serve some early-season strawberries with pouring cream. You'll probably need to sweeten them a touch at this time of year: slice and sprinkle them with caster sugar then leave them to macerate for 15–20 minutes before serving them.

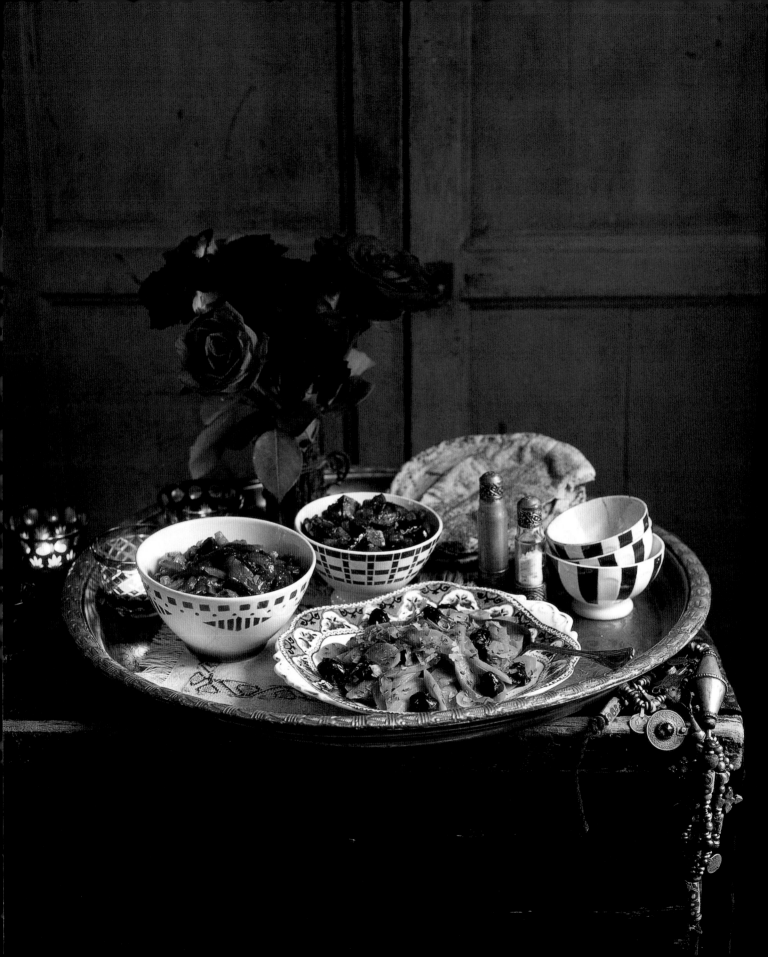

Moroccan-inspired summer supper

menu for 6

I love the gentle, subtle spicy flavours of Moroccan food, the exquisite balance between vegetables, meat, fruit and grain. The recipes are more time consuming to prepare than many in this book, admittedly, but this is a pleasurable meal to make with family or friends who share your passion for cooking.

∼

spiced carrot and black olive salad
aubergine and tomato salad
grilled pepper, tomato and chilli salad

chicken, lemon and green olive tagine

courgette and mint couscous

orange flower water salad

Moroccan mint tea and pastries

TO DRINK Most Moroccans do not drink alcohol, so a fruit juice like pomegranate juice would be an appropriate accompaniment to this meal, served in a large jug with ice and slices of lime. Wine-wise I'd go for a light, dry rosé such as a southern French Syrah rosé, a Spanish rosado or a mature oak-aged Spanish red like a Rioja Reserva.

The gentle aromatic spicing of these three Moroccan cooked salads is just perfect for a warm evening. You can prepare them well ahead. Serve with warmed flat breads or pitta bread.

spiced carrot and black olive salad

350 g young carrots

2 tablespoons olive oil

½ teaspoon Moroccan spice mix*

a pinch each of sea salt and sugar

75 g pitted black olives marinated with herbs

freshly squeezed juice of ½ orange (about 2 tablespoons)

a good squeeze of lemon juice

½ teaspoon lightly crushed roasted cumin seeds** (optional)

2 tablespoons chopped coriander

Serves 6

Cut the carrots into thin diagonal slices. Heat the oil in a saucepan over low heat, add the spice mix, and cook for a few seconds. Tip in the carrots, turn them in the spiced oil and cook gently for 3–4 minutes. Stir in the salt and sugar, add 2 tablespoons water and put a lid on the pan. Cook the carrots over low heat until they are soft (about 20 minutes), stirring occasionally and adding a little more water if the carrots start to burn.

Tip the carrots into a dish, cool, then mix in the olives and orange juice. Season to taste with salt and lemon juice. Just before serving, sprinkle over the cumin seeds, if using, and chopped coriander.

* I make my own Moroccan-style spice mix in small batches: 2 tablespoons each of ground cumin and ground coriander, 2 teaspoons turmeric and 1–1½ teaspoons chilli powder or hot (piquante) pimentón.

** To roast cumin seeds, put them in a small frying pan over a gentle heat and warm them through until they begin to change colour and smell fragrant.

aubergine and tomato salad

2 medium aubergines or 1 large (about 500 g)

4 tablespoons olive oil

1 onion, roughly chopped

1 garlic clove, crushed

2 tomatoes, skinned*, deseeded and diced

2 tablespoons chopped parsley

1 tablespoon chopped mint leaves

1–1½ tablespoons freshly squeezed lemon juice

1 teaspoon ground cumin

sea salt and freshly ground black pepper

a lidded wok

Serves 6

Slice off the aubergine stalks and cut each aubergine in half lengthways and then into cubes. Heat a wok for about 2 minutes over high heat, add the oil and heat for a few seconds, then tip in the aubergine cubes.

Stir-fry over medium heat for about 5 minutes until lightly browned, then turn the heat down slightly, add the onion and cook for another few minutes. Turn the heat down very low, stir in the garlic, cover the wok and cook gently for a further 10–12 minutes, stirring occasionally.

Tip the aubergine into a shallow dish and leave to cool for about 20 minutes. Mix in the tomato, parsley and mint. Season with the lemon juice and cumin and salt and pepper to taste.

grilled pepper, tomato and chilli salad

2 green peppers

3–4 Marmara or other long sweet peppers

400 g ripe tomatoes, skinned*

¼ teaspoon smoked sweet (dulce) pimentón or paprika

¼ teaspoon ground cumin

1 tablespoon freshly squeezed lemon juice

2 tablespoons olive oil

20 g pickled sliced Jalapeño chillies, rinsed and finely chopped

1 heaped tablespoon finely chopped parsley

sea salt and freshly ground black pepper

Serves 6

To skin the green and sweet peppers, either lay them over a low gas flame, turning frequently until the skins char, or halve them, lay them skin-side upwards on a grill pan and grill under high heat until the skins are blackened. Put the charred peppers in a bowl and cover with clingfilm. (This helps to loosen the skins.) Once the peppers are cool, rinse and rub them under cold running water, and the skins should slip off.

Deseed the peppers, slice them thickly and put in a serving bowl with the tomatoes. Measure the pimentón and cumin into another small bowl and whisk in the lemon juice and oil. Season to taste with salt and pepper. Pour the dressing over the peppers, add the Jalapeños and parsley and toss together.

*To skin the tomatoes, make a small cut near the stalk of each one with a sharp knife, put them in a heatproof bowl and pour over boiling water. Leave for a minute, then pour the water away and cover the tomatoes with cold water. The skins should peel off easily.

chicken, lemon, and green olive tagine

A fabulously fragrant chicken casserole that can be easily made ahead of time and reheated just before serving.

12 skinless, boneless chicken thighs (about 2¼ lbs. in total)
3 tablespoons olive oil
2 onions, sliced
2 garlic cloves, crushed
a good pinch of saffron threads
½ pint chicken or light vegetable stock
1 teaspoon finely grated fresh ginger or ½ teaspoon ground ginger
2 small preserved lemons
2½ oz. pitted green olives marinated with herbs
a small bunch of cilantro with its stalks
1–2 tablespoons freshly squeezed lemon juice
sea salt and freshly ground black pepper
1 teaspoon harissa paste, to serve (optional)*

a large cast-iron casserole or lidded skillet

Serves 6

Remove any excess fat from the chicken thighs and cut them in half. Heat the oil in the casserole or skillet, add the sliced onions and garlic and cook over medium heat for 7–8 minutes until the onions have started to soften and collapse. Add the chicken thighs, mix well with the onions and continue to cook for about 10 minutes over low heat, stirring occasionally. Put the saffron in a mortar or small bowl and crush with a pestle. Pour over 2 tablespoons of the stock and leave for a few minutes to infuse. Stir the saffron and ginger into the chicken. Quarter the preserved lemons, scoop out the flesh and finely sliced the peel. Halve the olives, add the olives and preserved lemon to the chicken. Pour in the remaining stock and mix well. Thoroughly wash the cilantro, cut off the stalks, tie them together with a piece of cotton or string and lay them in the casserole. Put a lid on the pan and leave to simmer until the

chicken is cooked (about another 30 minutes.) Remove the cilantro stalks and season the tagine to taste with lemon juice, salt and pepper. Put the harissa paste, if using, into a bowl, spoon off 4–5 tablespoons of the liquid from the tagine and mix with the harissa. Roughly chop the cilantro leaves, stir into the tagine and serve with the harissa on the side for those who like their food spicy!

* Harissa is a hot and spicy Moroccan chile paste.

zucchini and mint couscous

8 oz. zucchini
1 cup hot vegetable stock
9 oz. couscous
2 tablespoon olive oil
1 tablespoon finely chopped mint leaves
sea salt and freshly ground black pepper

Serves 6

Trim the ends off the zucchini and grate them coarsely. Pour the hot stock into a heatproof bowl and sprinkle over the couscous. Leave the grains until they have absorbed the liquid then fluff them up using a fork.

Heat the oil in a large skillet, tip in the grated zucchini and stir-fry for 1½ minutes until still bright green but beginning to soften. Tip in the chopped mint, then tip the zucchini into the couscous and fork through. Season to taste with salt and black pepper.

Time-saving tip: If you don't have time to make all the salads, you could serve a selection of raw vegetables including carrots, bell peppers, celery, radishes, and cucumber with a plain yogurt-based dip or Baba Ghanoush (a smoky eggplant purée.)

orange-flower water salad

Moroccans often serve oranges as a side salad, but I think they work particularly well as the refreshing end to a summer meal.

½ cup superfine or granulated sugar
6 oranges
1–2 teaspoons orange-flower water, to taste
freshly squeezed lemon juice, to taste
2 tablespoons chopped pistachios (optional)

Serves 6

Put the sugar in a saucepan with ¾ cup water and place it over low heat, stirring occasionally until all the sugar crystals have dissolved and the liquid is completely clear. Bring up to a boil and boil without stirring for 3–4 minutes, then turn off the heat and let cool. Using a sharp knife, score through the skin of each of the oranges, dividing them into quarters without cutting through the oranges themselves. Put in a large heatproof bowl, and pour over a kettleful of boiling water. Leave for a minute, then drain the water away and cover the oranges with cold water. Peel the oranges, removing as much of the white pith as possible. Slice the oranges across into thin slices, discarding any pips but carefully preserving the juice, then lay the orange slices in a bowl. Mix the cooled syrup with the reserved orange juice and 1 teaspoon orange-flower water and taste, adding a few more drops orange-flower water if you think it needs it or a squeeze of lemon juice if you find the syrup too sweet. Pour over the oranges, cover, and chill for at least a couple of hours. Sprinkle with the chopped pistachios (if using) and serve with a selection of Moroccan or Middle Eastern pastries (or hold them back to serve with the mint tea if you prefer.)

Moroccan mint tea

The ingredient that makes all the difference is the green tea which counteracts the overall sweetness of the tea.

2 small handfuls of mint leaves
2 green tea bags or 3 teaspoonfuls of loose green tea
2 teaspoons unrefined caster sugar

Makes 1 large pot or 6 cups

Put the mint leaves in a teapot along with the green tea and caster sugar. Pour over boiling water, stir and infuse for 4–5 minutes.

Serve the tea with a selection of shop-bought Moroccan or Middle-Eastern pastries.

a French bistro supper

menu for 6

A perfect menu for entertaining, as pretty well everything can be cooked in advance or assembled on the day. You don't necessarily need all the courses – the charcuterie would make a meal in itself, for instance, and you could skip the cheese – but it does make a wonderfully lavish spread. Given the all-French menu, it seems almost sacrilege to drink anything but French wine, although you could give it an unusual twist by serving red throughout.

gougères
TO DRINK A Beaujolais Kir would be a lovely way to kick off.

charcuterie and radishes
TO DRINK A Beaujolais would work well here.

boeuf bourguignon and pomme purée
TO DRINK A robust Rhône or Languedoc red.

sheeps' cheese with cherry compôte
TO DRINK Stay with your wine choice for the beef.

chocolate pots with Maury
TO DRINK A glass of sweet, red Maury from the South of France.

gougères

A classic French 'nibble' – just perfect with a Kir (see right).

50 g butter, cut into cubes
75 g strong white flour, sifted with ¼ teaspoon salt and a pinch of cayenne pepper
1 medium and 2 large eggs
50 g well-matured Gruyère cheese, grated finely

2 baking trays, lightly greased

Makes 20–24

Preheat the oven to 220°C (425°F) Gas 7. Measure 150 ml water into a saucepan and add the butter. Heat gently until the butter has melted, then bring to the boil. Remove from the heat. Add the sifted flour mixture. Beat vigorously until the mixture forms a ball and leaves the side of the pan clean. Set aside for 5 minutes. Beat 2 eggs and gradually add them to the pastry, working them in until the mixture is smooth and glossy. Add all except 1 heaped tablespoon of the cheese. Run the baking trays under the tap and then shake off any excess water. Place teaspoonfuls of the mixture onto each tray. Beat the remaining egg and brush the top of each puff lightly with a pastry brush. Sprinkle with the remaining cheese. Bake in the preheated oven for about 25 minutes until puffed up and golden. Remove the gougères from the oven and cut a small slit in the base of each to let the hot air escape. Cool on a wire rack.

Beaujolais Kir

1 x 50-cl bottle crème de cassis (blackcurrant-flavoured liqueur), chilled
2 x 75-cl bottles of Beaujolais Villages, chilled

Makes 12 glasses

Pour a good splash of crème de cassis into each glass and top up with the Beaujolais. Aim for about 1 part crème de cassis to 4 parts wine.

charcuterie and radishes

One of the easiest possible starters – which is why so many French bistros serve it. If you want to do it French-style buy some slices of air-dried ham, some whole saucisson and a thick slice of pâté or rillettes (which you can transfer to a small pottery bowl and pretend is your own!) Wash a couple of bunches of fresh radishes, cutting the leaves off a few centimetres above the base of the stem. Lay on some good French artisanal butter (the kind with salt crystals is perfect with this), some crusty baguette and a sharp Laguiole knife to cut the sausage. Almost a meal in itself!

boeuf bourguignon

Although Boeuf Bourguignon sounds as if it should be made from red Burgundy, I personally prefer to use a fuller-bodied red from the Rhône or Languedoc. I like to make it a day ahead to allow the flavours to develop, but it's not essential to do so.

900 g braising beef or steak

3 tablespoons olive oil

130 g cubed pancetta

3 onions, finely chopped

2 large garlic cloves, finely chopped

1½ tablespoons plain flour

450 ml full-bodied red wine, plus an extra splash if needed

a *bouquet garni* made from a few sprigs of thyme, parsley stalks and a bay leaf

25 g butter

250 g chestnut mushrooms, cleaned and halved

2 tablespoons finely chopped flat leaf parsley

salt and freshly ground black pepper

a large, flameproof casserole

Serves 6

Pat the meat dry, trim off any excess fat or sinew and cut into large chunks. Heat 1 tablespoon of the oil and fry the pancetta until lightly browned. Remove from the pan with a slotted spoon and transfer to a flameproof casserole. Brown the meat in 2 batches in the fat that remains in the pan and add to the bacon. Add the remaining oil and fry the onion slowly, covering the pan, until soft and caramelized (about 25 minutes), adding the chopped garlic halfway through the cooking time. Stir the flour into the onions, cook for a minute, then add the wine and bring to the boil. Pour over the meat, add the bouquet garni and bring back to the boil. Turn down the heat and simmer over very low heat for 2–2½ hours, until the meat is just tender. Turn off the heat and leave the casserole overnight.

The next day bring the casserole back to boiling point, then turn down low again. Heat the butter in a frying pan and fry the mushrooms until lightly browned (about 5 minutes). Tip the mushrooms into the stew, stir and cook for another 10–15 minutes. Season the casserole to taste with salt and pepper, adding an extra splash of wine if you don't think the flavour is quite pronounced enough. Sprinkle over chopped parsley before serving with pomme purée (see right) or boiled new potatoes.

pomme purée

This is the decadent French way of cooking mash.

1 kg red-skinned potatoes, such as Desirée or Wilja

50 ml double cream

75–100 ml whole milk

75 g unsalted butter, cut into cubes and at room temperature

sea salt and freshly ground black pepper

a potato ricer

Serves 6

Peel the potatoes and cut them into quarters or eighths (about half the size you would cut them for normal mash). Put them in a saucepan, pour over boiling water, add 1 teaspoon salt and bring back to the boil. Turn down the heat and simmer gently for about 12–15 minutes until you can easily pierce them with a skewer. Drain them in a colander, then return them to the pan over very low heat and leave them for a minute or 2 to dry off.

Mix the cream and milk together and heat until just below boiling point in a microwave or separate saucepan. Tip the potatoes back into the colander, then pass them through a potato ricer back into the pan. Pour in half the cream mixture and beat with a wooden spoon, then gradually beat in the remaining cream mixture and the butter. Season to taste with salt and pepper.

wine and chocolate

Chocolate isn't the easiest ingredient to match with wine, but a sweet red like Maury is generally much more successful than a sweet white. Other reds you could consider include Mavrodaphne of Patras from Greece, Banyuls, which like Maury is from the South of France, Recioto from Italy or late-bottled vintage port, especially if there are some dark berry fruits like cherries in the dessert. See also page 140.

chocolate pots with Maury

It's so easy to buy great chocolate puddings these days that if you're going to make them yourself you need to give them a bit of a twist. Here I've added the French red dessert wine Maury, a wonderful accompaniment for chocolate. It's very rich but chocoholics will probably want two!

200 g good-quality dark chocolate (minimum 70% cocoa solids)

150 ml Maury or 100 ml late-bottled vintage port

284-ml carton whipping cream

2 very fresh large organic egg yolks* (optional)

1–2 tablespoons unrefined caster sugar

sifted cocoa powder and icing sugar, to decorate

8–10 small ramekins or espresso cups

Serves 8–10

Break the chocolate into squares, put them in a food processor and briefly blitz them to break them into small pieces. Leave them in the processor.

Heat the Maury until almost boiling and pour it over the chocolate. Heat the cream, until almost boiling, and pour that over too. Leave for a few seconds to melt the chocolate, then whizz until the chocolate is smooth. Add the egg yolks and whizz again. Check for sweetness, adding caster sugar to taste. Pour the mixture into the serving dishes and chill in the fridge for a couple of hours, removing the desserts 20 minutes before serving. Using a small tea strainer, sift a thin layer of cocoa powder over the top of each pot, then follow with a sprinkling of icing sugar.

* This dessert contains raw egg. It improves the texture, but you could leave it out if you prefer.

sheeps' cheese with cherry compôte

Rather than a full cheeseboard, you could serve slices of sheeps' cheese as they do in the south-west of France with a good-quality bought cherry compôte, a combination that works much better with red wine than cheese alone. Serve with thin slices of sourdough or wholemeal bread.

a vegetarian harvest supper

menu for 6

This is a simple supper combining the best of autumn's produce with a couple of convenience products. Ready-rolled pastry has made it wonderfully easy to knock up a quick, impressive tart, while a simple dessert of baked or grilled fruit dresses up a bought tub of ice cream. The soup can even be made ahead and frozen if you like.

❧

pumpkin soup with honey and sage

TO DRINK Maybe I make a case for artisanal cider here? It is undergoing something of a renaissance at the moment. Or perry, which is cider made with pears. I'd pick a medium dry rather than a very dry one, which should take you right through the first two courses of this menu. Alternatively, choose a lightly oaked Chardonnay.

heirloom tomato, pepper and mozzarella tart

steamed new potatoes with butter, parsley and chives

garden salad

TO DRINK A cider or perry (see above), or a soft, fruity red like Merlot would work here.

grilled figs with cinnamon and sweet oloroso sherry
brandy snaps

TO DRINK As these desserts already include a full-bodied sweet sherry and are served with ice cream (which isn't the easiest ingredient to match with wine), I wouldn't suggest serving a dessert wine with either.

pumpkin soup with honey and sage

This is based on a delicious soup I had at a restaurant called Tom's Kitchen, run by top London chef Tom Aikens. His version, I discovered, contained chicken stock. Mine is vegetarian, but you could base it on chicken stock too.

75 g unsalted butter

1 small–medium onion, roughly chopped

1 carrot, finely chopped

1 garlic clove, crushed

1 kg pumpkin or butternut squash, deseeded, peeled and cut into cubes

2 heaped tablespoons clear honey

3 sprigs of sage, plus extra crisp-fried leaves (optional), to serve

750 ml vegetable stock

75 ml double cream

freshly squeezed lemon juice, to taste

sea salt and freshly ground black pepper

Serves 4–6

Gently melt the butter in a large lidded saucepan or flameproof casserole. Add the onion, carrot and garlic, stir, cover and cook over low heat for about 4–5 minutes. Add the cubed pumpkin, honey and sage, stir, replace the lid and continue to cook very gently for about 10 minutes. Pour in the stock, bring to the boil and cook for a further 10 minutes until the vegetables are soft. Turn off the heat and allow the soup to cool slightly, then remove the sage and strain the soup, retaining the liquid. Put half the cooked vegetables in a food processor with just enough of the reserved cooking liquid to blend into a smooth purée.

Transfer to a clean saucepan and repeat with the remaining vegetables, adding the purée to the first batch. Whizz the remaining liquid in the food processor to pick up the last bits of purée and add that too. Bring the soup slowly to the boil, then stir in the cream without boiling further. Season to taste with lemon juice (about 1 tablespoon), salt (about a teaspoon) and pepper.

Serve with an extra swirl of cream or scatter some crisp-fried sage leaves on top and serve with wholemeal or multigrain bread.

heirloom tomato, pepper and mozzarella tart

There are so many beautifully coloured tomatoes and peppers now, it's easy to make this spectacular-looking tart.

375-g sheet of ready-rolled puff pastry, thawed if frozen

1 large or 2 small red peppers

1 large or 2 small yellow peppers

3 tablespoons olive oil

2 garlic cloves, unpeeled and flattened

4 heaped tablespoons red pesto, homemade or from a jar

150 g buffalo mozzarella, drained and thinly sliced

125 g red cherry tomatoes, destalked and halved

125 g yellow cherry tomatoes, destalked and halved

$\frac{1}{2}$ teaspoon dried oregano or marjoram

1 egg, lightly beaten

25 g Parmesan cheese, grated or shaved

a few basil leaves, roughly torn

sea salt and freshly ground black pepper

a roasting tin

a rectangular baking tray, lightly greased

Serves 4–6

Preheat the oven to 200°C (400°F) Gas 6. Take the pastry out of the fridge at least 20 minutes before you need to unroll it. Quarter the peppers, remove the pith and seeds and cut each quarter into half lengthways. Put them in a roasting tin with the garlic cloves, pour over 2 tablespoons of the oil and mix together well. Roast for about 20–25 minutes until the edges of the peppers are beginning to blacken. Remove and let cool for 10 minutes.

Unroll the pastry and lay on the baking tray. Using a sharp knife, score a line around the pastry about 1¼ cm from the edge. Spread the pesto evenly inside the rectangle you've marked. Lay the pepper strips across the base of the tart, alternating red and yellow sections. Distribute the mozzarella pieces over the peppers. Season with black pepper. Arrange the halved tomatoes over the peppers, red on yellow and yellow on red. Sprinkle the oregano over the tart, season with a little salt and a little more pepper and trickle over the remaining oil. Turn the oven up to 220°C (425°F) Gas 7. Brush the edges of the tart with the egg and bake for 12 minutes or until the edge of the tart is well puffed up and beginning to brown. Turn the heat back down again to 200°C (400°F) Gas 6 and cook for another 12–15 minutes until the tops of the tomatoes are well browned. Sprinkle a little Parmesan over the tart, then leave to cool for 5 minutes. Scatter the basil over the tart to finish. Serve warm.

garden salad

One of the nicest things to have with a meal based on seasonal produce is a large, freshly picked salad of dark leafy greens, either from the garden or from your local farmers' market.

2 tablespoons seasoned rice vinegar

4 tablespoons sunflower oil

a pinch of sugar (optional)

200 g mixed dark leafy greens, such as rocket, spinach, chard and watercress

a few basil leaves (optional)

salt and freshly ground black pepper

Serves 6

Whisk together the rice vinegar and oil in a large salad bowl, adding extra salt and pepper to taste and the sugar it you like. Tip the greens into the salad dressing just before serving and toss everything together well.

steamed potatoes with butter, parsley and chives

Freshly dug potatoes have a wonderful earthy, nutty taste that's best shown off by steaming, as I've done here.

1 kg new or waxy salad potatoes, such as Charlotte

40 g butter, melted

2 heaped tablespoons chopped parsley

2 tablespoons finely snipped chives

sea salt and freshly ground black pepper

Serves 6

Scrub the potatoes, leaving the skins on, and cut into small, even-sized pieces. Steam until tender (about 7–8 minutes).

Put the potatoes in a serving dish, pour over the butter and sprinkle with the herbs. Season lightly with salt and black pepper and toss everything together. Serve warm.

grilled figs with cinnamon and sweet oloroso sherry

This is a very easy way to glam up a bought tub of toffee or caramel ice cream.

6 fresh ripe figs

2 tablespoons unrefined soft light brown sugar

1 teaspoon ground cinnamon

15 g unsalted butter

6 tablespoons sweet oloroso sherry

caramel or toffee ice cream, to serve

a medium ovenproof dish, buttered

Serves 6

Wash the figs carefully and pat dry. Halve and lay them cut-side up in a prepared ovenproof dish. Mix the sugar and cinnamon together and sprinkle over the figs. Put a knob of butter on top of each half fig and spoon over the sherry. Place the dish on the lowest grill level and grill until the butter and sugar have melted and the figs are beginning to caramelize (about 5–6 minutes). Serve with caramel or toffee ice cream, spooning over the warm syrup.

brandy snaps

This is one of those clever recipes that looks incredibly difficult but is in fact quite easy to follow.

2 tablespoons golden syrup

75 g unrefined soft light brown sugar

50 g unsalted butter

50 g plain flour, sifted with ½ teaspoon ground ginger and ¼ teaspoon ground allspice

2 large baking trays lined with non-stick baking parchment

Makes 12

Preheat the oven to 160°C (325°F) Gas 3. Measure out the golden syrup into a saucepan. (You'll find this easier to do if you dip the spoon into a jug of boiling water and shake off the excess before you put it in the tin). Add the sugar and butter and heat very gently until just melted, then take the pan off the heat. Don't allow the mixture to boil.

Mix the flour mixture thoroughly with the sugar, syrup and butter mixture. Put just 4 teaspoonfuls of the mixture on the first baking tray, allowing plenty of room for them to spread. Put in the preheated oven and cook for 8–10 minutes or until they are a rich brown. Five minutes later repeat with the second baking tray. (Baking the brandy snaps in batches gives you time to roll them up while they're still warm, otherwise they'll break rather than bend.) When you remove the first batch of biscuits, leave them to cool for a minute, then ease them off the paper with a palatte knife. If you want them the traditional curled-up brandy snap shape, roll them straightaway around the oiled handle of a wooden spoon, then place on a baking tray to cool. Otherwise, just leave them flat. Keep baking the mixture in batches of 4 until it is all used up. The brandy snaps will keep for 2–3 days in an airtight container.

it's cold outside
(a midwinter supper)

menu for 6

When it's cold outside, nothing is nicer than to sit around a candlelit table and enjoy a nice meal. This menu is full of warm, comforting flavours – a smooth vegetable soup, an old-fashioned pot roast served with gorgeous rich polenta and an indulgent, creamy dessert that's guaranteed to make you feel that the winter isn't so bad after all.

fennel, leek and cauliflower soup

TO DRINK Soup isn't the easiest dish to pair with wine (two liquids together don't always work) but the creamy texture of this soup goes well with a crisp, dry, fresh white such as a Chablis or other unoaked white Burgundy.

pot roast brisket with Zinfandel
roast pumpkin and garlic polenta with cavolo nero

TO DRINK You want a robust, warming red – a good Zinfandel or a Cabernet Sauvignon would be my top recommendations.

orange and Cointreau syllabub

TO DRINK I don't think this dessert needs an accompanying wine, but if you wanted to serve one, a small glass of Australian botrytized Semillon would work well.

fennel, leek and cauliflower soup

This deceptively creamy soup – which doesn't actually contain cream – is based on a delicious one made by Paul Hayes, the first chef at my son's London pub, The Marquess Tavern. Try if you can to use organic vegetables to make it: you really will be able to taste the difference.

2 tablespoons olive oil
25 g unsalted butter
2 leeks, trimmed and sliced
1 large or 2 small bulbs of fennel, trimmed and sliced (reserve the feathery leaves if they're still on the bulb)
1 large garlic clove, crushed
1 small or 1/2 large cauliflower
1 litre fresh chicken or vegetable stock or made with 1 organic stock cube
1 bay leaf
2–3 sprigs tarragon or 1 teaspoon dried tarragon
2–3 tablespoons whole milk (optional)
a small pinch of mace
sea salt and freshly ground white or black pepper
a few fennel, dill or parsley leaves and some chives, to garnish

Serves 6

Heat the oil for a minute or two in a large saucepan, then add the butter. When the foaming dies down, add the leeks, fennel and garlic, stir well, cover and cook over a low heat for about 8–10 minutes. Meanwhile, remove the florets from the cauliflower. Add them to the pan, stir and cook for another 3–4 minutes. Pour the stock over the vegetables, add the bay leaf and tarragon and bring to the boil. Partially cover the pan and simmer for about 15 minutes or until the cauliflower and fennel are soft. Remove from the heat and allow to cool slightly. Remove the bay leaf and tarragon. Strain the soup, reserving the liquid.

Put the vegetables in food processor and whizz until smooth, adding as much of the reserved liquid as you need to make a smooth, creamy consistency. Whizz the remaining liquid in the blender or food processor to pick up the last scraps of vegetable purée and add to the soup in the pan. Reheat gently, diluting the soup with a little more stock or milk if it seems too thick. Season to taste with salt, pepper and mace.

Chop the reserved fennel leaves or some dill or parsley and cut the chives into approximately 1 1/2-cm lengths. Serve the soup in individual bowls, scatter with the herbs and serve with some light rye or multigrain bread.

pot roast brisket with Zinfandel

Brisket is a much underrated cut with a rich flavour that lends itself well to braising. You can use any full-bodied red, but Zinfandel has just the right gutsy rustic character.

200 ml Zinfandel or other full-bodied red wine
200 ml fresh beef stock or stock made with 1/2 a stock cube, cooled
2 tablespoons red wine vinegar
1 large garlic clove, crushed
1 bay leaf
1 onion, chopped
a few of sprigs of thyme or 1/2 teaspoon dried thyme
1.5 kg boned, rolled brisket of beef
2–3 tablespoons sunflower or light olive oil
2 tablespoons dry Marsala or Madeira
sea salt and freshly ground pepper

a flameproof casserole

Serves 6

Mix the wine and stock with the wine vinegar, garlic, bay leaf, onion and thyme. Put the meat in a sturdy plastic bag, pour over the marinade and pull the top of the bag together tightly so that the liquid covers the meat. Knot the top of the bag or seal with a wire tie. Leave the meat to marinate in the fridge for at least 4 hours or overnight.

Preheat the oven to 200°C (400°F) Gas 6. Remove the meat from the marinade and dry thoroughly with kitchen paper. Strain the marinade and reserve the liquid. Heat the oil in a flameproof casserole. Brown the meat all over in the hot oil then add 3–4 tablespoons of the strained marinade. Put a lid on the casserole and roast for 2 hours. Check from time to time that the pan juices are not burning. Add more marinade if necessary, but the flavour of this dish comes from the well-browned sticky juices, so do not add too much extra liquid. If on the other hand more liquid has formed, spoon some out. Simmer the remaining marinade over low heat until it loses its raw, winey taste.

Once the meat is cooked, set it aside in a warm place. Spoon any fat off the surface of the pan juices and add the Marsala and the cooked marinade. Bring to the boil, scraping off all the brown tasty bits from the side of the casserole and adding a little extra water if necessary. Season to taste with salt and pepper and serve spooned over slices of the meat or in a gravy boat for pouring.

roast pumpkin and garlic polenta

Polenta normally has lavish amounts of butter and cheese added to give it flavour, but here's a much lighter version made with roast pumpkin and roast garlic, which you can cook at the same time as the beef (see page 105).

1 medium pumpkin or 1 large
butternut squash

5 large garlic cloves, unpeeled

3 tablespoons sunflower or grapeseed oil

40 g butter

50 g Parmesan cheese, grated, plus
extra to taste

1.2 litres vegetable stock, plus a little
extra as necessary

250 g good-quality Italian polenta

sea salt and freshly ground black pepper

a large roasting tin

Serves 6

Preheat the oven to 190°C (375°F) Gas 5. Halve the pumpkin. Cut one half into quarters and scoop out the seeds. Quarter the other half, scoop out the seeds, cut each quarter into 2 or 3 pieces and cut away the skin with a sharp knife. Put all the pumpkin in a roasting tin along with the garlic cloves. Drizzle with the oil, mix well together and season generously with salt and pepper. Roast in the preheated oven for about 35–40 minutes until soft.

Remove the quartered pumpkin from the tin and set the rest aside to be reheated just before serving. Scrape the flesh off the skin and place in a food processor. Pop the roasted garlic cloves out of their skins and add to the pumpkin and whizz until smooth. Add the butter and Parmesan, whizz again and season with salt and pepper. Cook the polenta in the vegetable stock, following the instructions on the packet, taking care to whisk well to avoid lumps. Add the pumpkin and garlic purée to the cooked polenta and mix well. Add a little extra stock if needed to give a slightly sloppy consistency. Check the seasoning,

adding more salt, pepper and Parmesan to taste. Reheat the pumpkin pieces briefly in a microwave or frying pan. Serve topped with pumpkin pieces.

cavolo nero

3 heads of cavolo nero or spring greens

3 tablespoons olive oil

1 garlic clove, thinly sliced

sea salt and freshly ground black pepper

Serves 6

Pull the leaves off the stalks and tear out the central tough rib of each leaf. Slice the greens and put in a saucepan. Pour over just enough boiling water to cover, bring back to the boil and cook for 2–3 minutes. Drain the greens. Add the oil to the saucepan and cook the garlic very gently without colouring until soft and sweet (about 5 minutes). Toss the greens in the garlic-flavoured oil and cook over low heat for 5 minutes. Season to taste and serve.

orange and Cointreau syllabub

Syllabub – a delicious, velvety smooth concoction of sweet wine and cream – is one of the great English desserts, dating from the 16th century. I like it made with orange rather than lemon and topped with an irresistibly crunchy mixture of orange zest and sugar.

150 ml southern French Muscat or other strong sweet white wine (minimum 15% ABV)

1 tablespoon Cointreau or other orange-flavoured liqueur

finely grated zest of 2 unwaxed oranges

2 tablespoons freshly squeezed orange juice

2 tablespoons freshly squeezed lemon juice

4 tablespoons unrefined caster sugar

400 ml double cream, chilled

a large bowl, chilled for 30–40 minutes in the fridge or for 15–20 minutes in the freezer

6 small glass tumblers or dishes

Serves 6

Pour the wine into a bowl, add the Cointreau, half the grated orange zest, the orange and lemon juice and 2 tablespoons of the sugar. Stir, cover and refrigerate for several hours or overnight. Strain through a fine sieve. Pour the cream into the chilled bowl and beat with an electric hand-held whisk until it starts to thicken. Gradually add the orange-flavoured wine, beating between each addition until the cream thickens again. (Don't overbeat it, or it will separate.) Aim for a thick pouring consistency. When the final addition of wine has been incorporated, the mixture should hold a trail when you lift out the beaters, but shouldn't be stiff.) Ladle the mixture into tumblers and chill for at least an hour before serving. In the meantime, mix the remaining orange zest and sugar, and leave it on a plate to crisp up. Just before serving, sprinkle the orange sugar over the top of each glass.

a romantic Champagne dinner

menu for 2

The key to a romantic dinner is not to give yourself too much last-minute work or to eat or drink too much – unless you want to end up snoring on the sofa! Since you're probably going to open a bottle of Champagne at some point, you might as well drink it all the way through, which works well with this luxurious seafood-based menu.

~

warm scallop salad
with crispy pancetta and parsnip crisps
or
warm oysters with cucumber and Champagne

lobster and chips

Chaource with black truffles

passion fruit pavlovas

TO DRINK This menu is designed to be accompanied by Champagne and, if you can run to it, a vintage one. Choose a recent vintage rather than a very old one, as you may not like the complex yeasty flavours that mature Champagne acquires. An alternative would be to drink a glass of fizz with the oysters or scallops and move on to a top-quality Chardonnay with the lobster.

warm scallop salad with crispy pancetta and parsnip crisps

Scallops are one of my favourite foods – so quick to cook. Try and buy diver-caught ones if you can find them.

1 parsnip

6 large fresh scallops

1 tablespoon olive oil plus a little extra for dressing the salad

60 g cubed pancetta

4 tablespoons full-bodied dry white wine, such as a Chardonnay or Viognier

2 tablespoons fish stock or water

1 tablespoon double cream or crème fraîche

a small bag of mixed leaf salad (about 80 g)

sea salt and freshly ground black pepper

vegetable oil, for frying

a wok

Serves 2

First make the parsnip crisps. Peel the parsnip and cut off the bottom end to leave you with a piece about 10 cm long and 3–4 cm wide at its narrowest point. Shave off fine slices using a mandoline or vegetable peeler. Fill a wok about one-quarter full with vegetable oil and heat until very hot. Fry the parsnip crisps in batches, a few at a time, removing them as they brown with a slotted spoon and drain them on kitchen paper. Sprinkle them lightly with salt.

Season the scallops on both sides with salt and black pepper. Heat a frying pan and add the olive oil. Fry the pancetta until crisp, then remove it from the pan with a slotted spoon and pour off the fat. Return the frying pan to the hob, reheat for a minute until almost smoking, then lay the scallops in the pan. Cook them for 1–1½ minutes, depending how thick they are, then turn them over and cook for the same amount of time the other side. Set aside and keep warm. Pour the white wine into the pan, let it bubble up and reduce it by half. Add the fish stock and keep bubbling away until you have just over a couple of tablespoons of juice altogether. Return any juices that have accumulated under the scallops to the pan and stir in the cream. Check the seasoning, adding pepper to taste and a little more salt if necessary, warm through for a few seconds, then turn off the heat.

Put half the salad leaves on each plate and scatter over the pancetta. Drizzle with a little olive oil and season lightly. Arrange the most attractive parsnip crisps over the top. Lay 3 scallops on each plate and spoon the pan juices over them. Serve immediately.

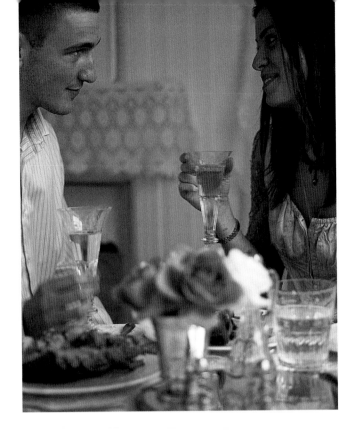

warm oysters with cucumber and Champagne

75-g chunk of cucumber, thinly peeled, deseeded and diced

150 ml dry Champagne

1–2 shallots, sliced

8 fresh oysters

3 tablespoons double cream

a knob of butter

salt and freshly ground black pepper

a few leaves of snipped dill, to garnish

Serves 2

Sprinkle the diced cucumber lightly with salt and cover with a weighted plate for 20 minutes. Meanwhile, pour the Champagne into a small saucepan with the shallots, bring to the boil and reduce until there are just a couple of tablespoons of liquid. Remove the shallots. Open the oysters, pouring off the liquor and setting it aside. Add the cream to the Champagne and cook until you have a coating consistency. Rinse the cucumber thoroughly and pat dry. Strain the oyster liquor, then add it to the pan. Heat through and whisk in the butter. Add the oysters and cucumber and reheat gently for about 1–1½ minutes until the oysters are just firm. Take off the heat. Rinse and dry the oyster shells, then divide the oysters and cucumber between them. Sprinkle with a little dill and serve.

lobster and chips

Since dealing with a live lobster is possibly not the most relaxing prelude to a romantic evening, I suggest you buy a cooked one!

1 medium–large cooked lobster

60 g butter

2 garlic cloves, crushed

freshly squeezed juice of 1 small lime (about 2 tablespoons)

1 teaspoon grated fresh ginger

14–16 basil leaves, finely shredded

sea salt and cayenne pepper

a baking dish

lobster crackers or mallet

Serves 2

Put the lobster underside downwards on a chopping board and cut through it vertically with a large sharp knife. Carefully extract the white lobster meat from the tail, removing the long, thin membrane near the back. Remove the claws and crack them with lobster crackers or hit them smartly with a mallet. Carefully remove the meat, breaking it up as little as possible. Pick out any remaining white meat from the shell, scrape out the rest and discard. Cut the lobster meat into large chunks.

Melt the butter gently in a saucepan and stir in the garlic, lime juice and ginger. Add the lobster pieces and warm through for a minute or 2 without boiling. Add the basil and season with salt and cayenne pepper. Carefully transfer the empty shells to the baking dish and reassemble the lobster meat in the shells. Put the dish under a preheated hot grill for 2–3 minutes until you can hear the lobster meat begin to sizzle.

Serve with a few hand-cut chips or baby new potatoes.

passion fruit pavlovas

A simple-to-assemble, fresh-tasting and impressive dessert.

2 passion fruit

1 tablespoon freshly squeezed orange juice

1 teaspoon unrefined caster sugar, plus extra to taste

a few drops of orange flower water (optional)

2 bought meringue nests

2 heaped tablespoons lemon or orange curd (optional)

4 small scoops good-quality vanilla ice cream

Serves 2

Halve the passion fruit and scoop the pulp and seeds into a small bowl, taking care not to remove any of the bitter pith.

Add the orange juice and sugar and stir. Check for sweetness, adding the orange flower water and/or extra sugar to taste.

Put a meringue nest on each plate and spoon the curd, if using, into the base. Top with the vanilla ice cream and spoon over the orange and passion fruit sauce.

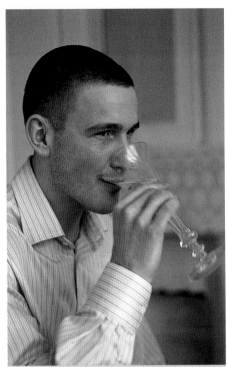

Chaource with black truffle

This is a brilliant tip I got from American cookery writer Patricia Wells. Take a small, deep, round, soft white rinded cows' cheese, about 7 cm in diameter and about 4–5 cm deep or half a slightly bigger one, such as Chaource (which comes from the Champagne region), and cut it horizontally into three slices (this is easier if it's chilled). Thinly slice a black truffle, lay the slices between the layers, trickling over a few drops of black truffle-infused oil over the sliced truffles, and sandwich the layers together. Wrap tightly with clingfilm and refrigerate for at least a day and preferably two days. Cut into wedges, bring to room temperature and serve with slices of sourdough or baguette.

food and fizz

Sparkling wine is much more versatile with food than people think, its natural carbonation acting as a palate cleanser and appetite stimulant. Its lightness makes it a natural partner for raw or lightly cooked shellfish and other seafood, for light pastas and risottos, and with chicken. Surprisingly, although it is regarded as a dry wine, you can also drink it with airy desserts such as gâteaux, soufflés and meringues, and with red berry fruits such as strawberries and raspberries. You can also drink it with light creamy cheeses such as Chaource.

a festive winter supper

menu for 6

Most of us have tried and trusted recipes for our Christmas or Thanksgiving dinner from which we wouldn't dare deviate, but there are many other meals to be catered for during the holiday season. They needn't be (thankfully) as time-consuming to prepare as The Big Meal itself, but they can be a lot more fun for the cook. You can mix and match the courses any way you like: follow the soup with the pumpkin pie or with biscuits and mulled wine, or simply invite a few friends round for some egg nog and biscuits.

chestnut and Puy lentil soup
with whipped celeriac cream

TO DRINK Choose a light unoaked Chardonnay such as Chablis or a neutral clean white such as Albariño. (If you don't make the celeriac topping, you could use a richer, oakier Chardonnay.)

winter cheeseboard (see page 138)

roast pumpkin and pecan pie

TO DRINK Muscats and Moscatels go particularly well with pumpkin pie – Australian liqueur Muscat if you have an exceptionally sweet tooth, a lighter Southern French or Spanish Muscat if you haven't. You could also try a sweet sherry or a young tawny port.

ginger and cinnamon biscuits
orange-mulled wine, mulled cider or egg nog

chestnut and Puy lentil soup with whipped celeriac cream

This is a spectacularly rich, satisfying soup with a light-as-air, foamy topping. You can prepare the soup ahead and it's a particularly good way to use up a tasty turkey or ham stock. You don't have to peel your own chestnuts, but they do taste wonderful and it's a nice, cosy thing to do if you've got company in the kitchen. If you prefer to serve the soup on its own without the topping, save some of the chopped chestnut for garnishing, frying the pieces in a little butter before serving.

450 g whole chestnuts or 350 g ready-prepared chestnuts

4 tablespoons light olive oil

1 leek, trimmed and thinly sliced

1 large carrot, finely diced

1 celery stick, thinly sliced

1 garlic clove, crushed

1 teaspoon sweet (dulce) pimentón or paprika

1.5–1.75 litres fresh turkey, duck, ham, chicken or game stock or stock made with 2 organic beef or chicken cubes

175 g green Puy lentils, rinsed

2 tablespoons dry Marsala, Madeira or amontillado sherry

½–1 teaspoon Worcestershire or dark soy sauce (optional)
sea salt and freshly ground black pepper

For the celeriac cream:

500 g celeriac

568 ml semi-skimmed milk

25 g butter

freshly grated nutmeg, to taste

a few snipped chives, to garnish

Serves 6–8

Wash the chestnuts and make a cut with a sharp knife in the curved side of each one. Put in a saucepan of boiling water, bring back to the boil and boil for 3 minutes. Turn the heat off and remove the chestnuts 2 at a time, letting them cool for a few seconds, then peeling off both the hard outer shell and inner brown papery skin. If they become harder to peel, bring the water back to the boil again. Chop the chestnuts roughly.

Heat the oil in a large saucepan, add the leek, carrot and celery, stir well and cook over medium heat until the vegetables start to soften (about 5–6 minutes). Stir in the garlic and pimentón and cook for a minute, then add the chestnuts and 1 litre of the stock and bring to the boil. Add the lentils to the vegetables, then cook for about 35–40 minutes until the vegetables are soft. Cool for 10 minutes, then pass the soup in batches through a food processor. Return the soup and remaining stock to the pan, add the Marsala and reheat gently. Add more stock if necessary and season to taste with salt, pepper and Worcestershire sauce.

Meanwhile, to make the celeriac cream, remove the tough outer skin from the celeriac and cut it into cubes. Put in a saucepan, add enough of the milk to cover and bring to the boil. Partially cover the pan and simmer for about 20–25 minutes, until the celeriac is soft. Remove the celeriac with a slotted spoon, leaving the liquid behind, and whizz it in a food processor. Season with salt, pepper and a little freshly grated nutmeg. Remove half the purée and add half the remaining milk to the purée in the food processor. Whizz until smooth, light and foamy, adding the extra milk if needed.

Serve the soup in bowls with a generous swirl of celeriac purée on the top and garnish with snipped chives. Serve with some crusty sourdough or multigrain bread.

roast pumpkin and pecan pie

This recipe may look slightly daunting, but I promise you it is worth the effort. Do roast the pumpkin if you're cooking it from scratch – it has a much better texture than when you boil it.

For the pastry:
250 g plain flour
1 teaspoon ground ginger
2 tablespoons icing sugar
110 g butter, chilled and cut into cubes
25 g white vegetable fat or shortening
1 egg yolk (reserve the white)
a pinch of salt

For the pumpkin purée:
500 g pumpkin flesh (see method)
1 tablespoon bourbon or dark rum
1 tablespoon light muscovado sugar
¼ teaspoon mixed spice
15 g butter, chilled

For the pie filling:
100 g light muscovado sugar
1 tablespoon maple syrup or clear honey
1½ teaspoons mixed spice
½ teaspoon ground cinnamon
a pinch of salt
1 tablespoon bourbon or dark rum
3 eggs
2 tablespoons plain flour, sifted
150 ml double cream

For the topping:
50 g pecan nuts
1 tablespoon light muscovado sugar

a flan tin 23 cm across and 3.5 cm deep

Serves 6

First make the pastry. Sift the flour, ginger and icing sugar into a large bowl. Cut the butter and fat cubes into the flour, then rub lightly with your fingertips until the mixture resembles coarse breadcrumbs. Mix the egg yolk with 2 tablespoons ice-cold water, add to the bowl, mix lightly and pull together into a ball, adding extra water if needed. Shape into a flat disc, put in a plastic bag and refrigerate for at least half an hour.

Preheat the oven to 200°C (400°F) Gas 6. To make the pumpkin purée, scrape away all the pumpkin seeds and fibrous flesh surrounding them and cut into even-sized chunks. Put the chunks on a piece of lightly oiled foil. Sprinkle over the bourbon, sugar and mixed spice and dot with the chilled butter. Bring the foil up round the sides and fold over carefully to form a loose but airtight package. Place in a baking dish and cook in the preheated oven for 40 minutes until the pumpkin is soft. Carefully open up the foil, let cool for a few minutes, then tip the pumpkin and the juices into a food processor and whizz until smooth.

Roll out the pastry and lower into the flan tin. Trim the edges and press the base well into the tin. Prick lightly with a fork and chill for another half an hour. Cover the pastry case with foil and weight down with baking beans. Bake at 200°C (400°F) Gas 6 for about 12 minutes, then remove the foil and beans, brush the base of the pastry with the reserved egg white to seal it and return to the oven for about 3–4 minutes. Remove it from the oven and lower the temperature to 190°C (375°F) Gas 5.

Add the sugar and maple syrup to the pumpkin purée, then the spices, salt and bourbon. Add the eggs, one by one, beating them in well, then sift in the flour and mix lightly. Finally, add the cream and pour the filling into the flan case. Put the tin on a baking tray, transfer to the oven and bake for about 50 minutes until the filling is just set and firm, reducing the temperature to 180°C (350°F) Gas 4 after 25 minutes.

About 10 minutes before the end of the cooking time, chop the pecan nuts finely (by hand). Put them in a saucepan with the sugar and warm gently until the sugar starts to melt. About 5 minutes before the tart is cooked sprinkle the nuts evenly over the surface of the tart and return it to the oven for 5 minutes. Remove from the oven and let cool for 20 minutes before cutting. Serve lukewarm with lightly whipped cream.

ginger and cinnamon biscuits

It's easy enough to buy Christmassy biscuits, but it's worth baking them yourself if only for the gorgeous smell that permeates the kitchen. This recipe is adapted from one in an old cookery book called 'Cooking for Christmas' by Shona Crawford Poole, first published in 1980.

90 g dark muscovado sugar

110 g soft butter, cut into cubes

6 tablespoons golden syrup

100 ml double cream

375 g plain flour

1 tablespoon ground ginger

1 tablespoon ground cinnamon

⅛ teaspoon ground cloves (optional)

1 teaspoon baking powder

½ teaspoon salt

2 baking trays lined with non-stick baking parchment

star-shaped biscuit cutters in various sizes (or any other shapes you like, such as Christmas trees, bells etc).

Makes about 40 biscuits

Sift the sugar through a coarse sieve to remove any lumps and put in a large bowl with the cubed butter. Beat together until smooth, then beat in the golden syrup and cream. Measure out the flour, add the ginger, cinnamon, cloves, baking powder and salt and sift into another bowl. Add the flour and spice mixture to the creamed mixture a third at a time until you have a stiff dough. Form the dough into a flat disc, wrap in foil and refrigerate for at least 3 hours.

When you're ready to bake the biscuits preheat the oven to 190°C (375°F) Gas 5. Cut off a quarter of the dough, flour your work surface and rolling pin generously and roll out the dough thinly. Stamp out shapes with your cutters. Carefully prise them off the work surface with a palate knife, lay them on one of the baking trays and bake for about 8 minutes. Leave them to firm up for 2–3 minutes, then transfer to a wire rack until crisp. Repeat with the remaining pieces of dough, re-rolling the offcuts to give you as many biscuits as possible. The biscuits will keep in an airtight container for up to one week.

orange-mulled wine

If you've never made mulled wine yourself, you should try. It couldn't be simpler and tastes infinitely better than the ready-mixed versions. The only thing you have to be careful about is that the wine doesn't boil.

2 x 75-cl bottles of medium-bodied fruity red wine

1 orange studded with cloves, plus a few orange slices to serve

thinly pared zest of ½ an unwaxed lemon

2 cinnamon sticks

6 cardamom pods, lightly crushed

a little freshly grated nutmeg or a small pinch of ground nutmeg

100 g soft brown sugar

100 ml orange-flavoured liqueur, such as Cointreau or Grand Marnier, or brandy

Makes 14–16 small cups or glasses

Pour the wine into a large saucepan with 500 ml cold water. Add the orange, lemon zest, spices and sugar and heat gently until almost boiling. Turn down to the lowest possible heat so that the liquid barely trembles and simmer for half an hour to allow the spices to infuse thoroughly. Add the orange-flavoured liqueur then reheat gently. Strain into a large, warmed bowl and float a few thin slices of orange on top. Ladle into small cups or glasses and serve with mince pies.

mulled cider

This makes such a delicious alternative to mulled wine that I'm not sure that I don't like it even better!

500 ml traditional dry cider
125 ml Calvados (French apple brandy) or brandy
750 ml cloudy apple juice
75 g soft brown sugar
a thinly pared strip of lemon zest
2 cinnamon sticks
8 cloves
6 even-sized slices of dried apple, halved, to garnish

Makes 10–12 glasses

Put the cider, Calvados and apple juice in a large saucepan. Add the sugar, lemon zest, cinnamon sticks and cloves and heat very gently until the sugar has dissolved. Heat until almost boiling, then turn off the heat, add the halved, dried apple slices and leave the pan for half an hour for the flavours to infuse. Reheat the punch again, taking care not to boil it and serve in heatproof cups or glasses with a slice of the apple in each.

egg nog

Once you've tasted this delicious light, foamy punch, I suspect you'll want to make it every year. This version is adapted from a recipe in top American bartender Dale Degroff's 'The Craft of the Cocktail'.

3 very fresh large organic eggs
75 g unrefined caster sugar
100 ml bourbon
100 ml spiced rum
570 ml whole milk
275 ml whipping cream
a whole nutmeg, for grating

Serves 6–8

Separate the egg yolks carefully from the whites and put them in separate large bowls. Beat the egg yolks with an electric hand-held whisk, gradually adding 50 g of the sugar, until they turn light in colour and moussey in texture. Beat in the bourbon and spiced rum, then stir in the milk and cream.

Clean and dry your whisk thoroughly then whisk the egg whites until beginning to stiffen. Add the remaining sugar to the whites and whisk until they form a soft peak. Fold the whites into the egg nog mixture and grate over a little nutmeg.

Ladle out the egg nog into small glasses or cups. Have teaspoons available for those who prefer to spoon rather than sip it.

a Chinese New Year supper

menu for 4

The Chinese New Year is one of those annual events that just captures the imagination.
It is celebrated in such a colourful and joyous way and Chinese food is so delicious,
quick and simple to make that we all feel inspired to have a go at it. This is a menu
where you could easily buy in the dim sum and even the dessert (though this one is fun
to make) but do have a go at the really delicious seafood stir-fry.

sesame prawn toasts and other dim sum

TO DRINK I've discovered that a good cold gin and tonic is exceptionally refreshing with fried
dim sum, such as prawn toasts and spring rolls.

luxury seafood stir-fry

with steamed pak choi

TO DRINK There are two ways to go with the wine for Chinese food – an aromatic white such as
Riesling (I would recommend a young dry one from Germany or Alsace), or a fruity Bordeaux rosé,
which works surprisingly well.

stem ginger and almond ice cream, mandarin oranges
and fortune cookies

TO DRINK Finish with a cup of delicate jasmine or chrysanthemum tea.

a selection of dim sum

Frankly, I think life is too short to make your own dim sum, so unless you're already an expert at rolling miniature spring rolls and making featherlight steamed dumplings, I would order them in from your local takeaway or buy them ready-made. The exception are these simple sesame prawn toasts, which are much easier to handle than the classic Chinese deep-fried ones and can be prepared ahead and baked at the last minute.

sesame prawn toasts

350 g cooked, shelled prawns
2–3 spring onions, trimmed and finely chopped
1 teaspoon finely grated fresh ginger or ginger paste
1 teaspoon finely grated fresh garlic or garlic paste
1½ teaspoons Vietnamese or Thai fish sauce
2 teaspoons light soy sauce
¼ teaspoon sesame oil
1 egg white
1 tablespoon ground rice
a pinch of caster sugar
about 5 thin slices of white bread, preferably 2–3 days old
60–75 g sesame seeds
sea salt and freshly ground black pepper

2 non-stick baking trays

Makes about 30 toasts

Put the prawns in a food processor along with all the other ingredients, except the bread and sesame seeds, and whizz until smooth. Transfer to a bowl, cover and refrigerate for an hour or 2 for the flavours to mellow.

Preheat the oven to 230°C (450°F) Gas 8. Cut the crusts off the bread and toast lightly. Let cool, then spread each slice thickly with the prawn paste. Cut each slice into 6. Put the sesame seeds in a shallow bowl. Press the prawn toasts upper-side down lightly into the sesame seeds, then lay them on the baking trays. Bake in the preheated oven for about 5–6 minutes until the toasts are warm and the sesame seeds lightly browned. Let cool for 10 minutes before serving.

luxury seafood stir-fry

This recipe may look complicated, but it's simply a matter of assembling the ingredients and throwing them together at the last minute in a wok.

400 g large prawns, thawed if frozen
200 g fresh queen (small) scallops
1 tablespoon cornflour
3 tablespoons sunflower or light olive oil
4–6 spring onions, trimmed and thinly sliced
125 g shiitake mushrooms, wiped and thinly sliced
200 g broccoli, cut into small florets
1 garlic clove, crushed
1 knob of fresh ginger, about 2.5 cm square, peeled and grated
½ teaspoon Sichuan pepper or crushed chillies (optional)
sea salt and freshly ground white pepper

For the sauce:

225 ml light vegetable stock
freshly squeezed juice of 1 large lemon (about 3–4 tablespoons)
3–4 tablespoons rice wine, sake or fino sherry
1 tablespoon caster sugar
1 tablespoon light soy sauce (or 1½ teaspoons dark soy sauce)
1 rounded teaspoon cornflour

a wok

Serves 4–6

Reserve any liquid from the prawns and scallops. Pat them dry with kitchen paper and put in a large bowl. Sprinkle over the cornflour, season with 1 teaspoon salt and ½ teaspoon white pepper and toss thoroughly, then cover and set aside (in the fridge if you're preparing the dish more than half an hour in advance). Microwave or blanch the broccoli in boiling, salted water for 2 minutes. Drain and set aside.

To make the sauce, combine the stock in a jug with the lemon juice and 3 tablespoons of the rice wine. Stir in the sugar and soy sauce and check the seasoning, adding more rice wine or other ingredients to taste. Mix the cornflour with 1 tablespoon water.

When you're ready to cook, heat the wok, add the oil and tip in the spring onions and mushrooms. Stir-fry for 2 minutes, then add the broccoli, garlic and ginger. Stir-fry for another minute then season with Sichuan pepper, if using. Tip in the seafood, the sauce and any liquid from the prawns and scallops and cook, stirring, until it comes to the boil (about 3 minutes). Add the cornflour mixture and stir until thickened. Remove from the heat and check the seasoning, adding extra salt or pepper if needed. Serve with steamed pak choi.

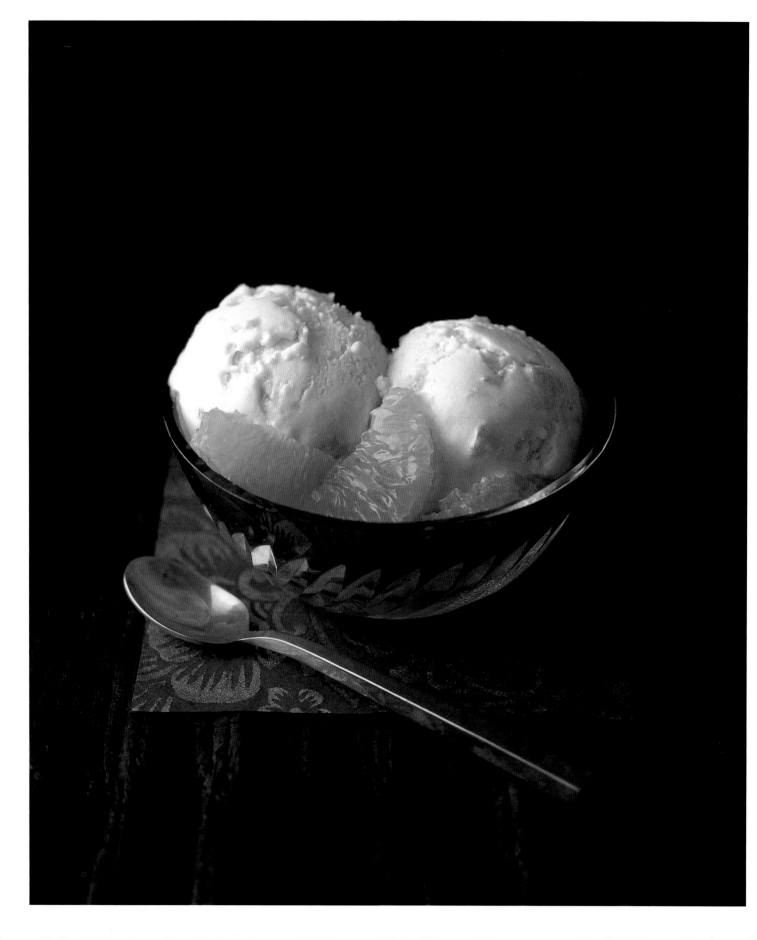

stem ginger and almond ice cream

You can make this luxurious ice cream milder or stronger, depending how much ginger you use. I've given quantities for four people, as it'll fit into a standard ice cream machine. Just make the recipe twice to serve six to eight.

4–6 pieces of stem ginger, plus 3 tablespoons of syrup from the jar

150 ml ginger wine, such as Stone's

1 tablespoon orange-flavoured liqueur, such as Cointreau, plus extra to serve

300-g carton fresh ready-made custard

142-ml carton whipping cream

a few drops of almond extract, to taste

fortune cookies and canned mandarin oranges, to serve

Serves 4

Chop the ginger very finely and put in a bowl. Put the syrup in a small saucepan with the ginger wine and Cointreau, bring to the boil and simmer for about 8–10 minutes until the liquid has reduced by about half. Pour over the ginger and let cool for 10 minutes.

Transfer the custard to a large bowl and stir in the ginger and syrup. Whip the cream lightly and fold it into the custard, then almond extract to taste. Pour the custard into an ice cream machine and churn until firm, following the manufacturer's instructions. Or, if you don't have a machine, pour the mixture into a shallow, freezerproof container and put in the freezer, then remove after 1½ hours and whisk with an electric hand-held whisk. Repeat this freezing and whisking process 2 more times, then leave until thoroughly frozen. Store the frozen ice cream in a sealed plastic box and freeze for 24 hours.

Transfer the ice cream to the fridge for 30 minutes before serving to make it easier to scoop. Serve with fortune cookies, or another light crisp biscuit, and mandarin oranges, drained and marinated in 2 tablespoons orange-flavoured liqueur. Do give each person 8 segments – 8 is a sacred number in China and considered to bring luck and prosperity!

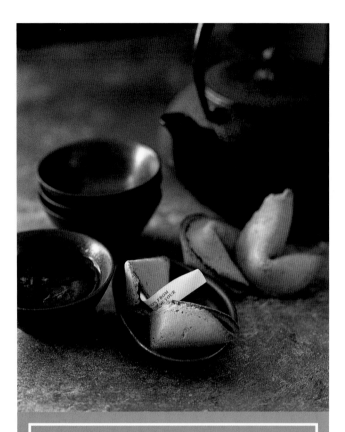

tea in China

Tea is so much a part of life in China that it is drunk at almost any time of day – though rarely with meals. For the most part it is 'green' or unfermented tea, sometimes served on its own, sometimes infused with jasmine petals. There is a delightful ritual to the whole preparation and consumption that is repetitive and soothing. It's well worth seeking out fine teas, many of which can now be bought on-line, and acquiring delicate porcelain bowls in which to serve them. The temperature and source of the water is also critical to the flavour and leaves should not be steeped for too long a time.

a quick deli supper

menu for 4

Sometimes you want to have friends round midweek. Most times you don't have time to cook. Solution? A visit to your local deli, where you can easily source the ingredients for this simple, throw-it-together menu. All you have to do on the night is make a creamy mushroom risotto, which you can stir while you chat to your friends in the kitchen. My cocktail desserts are also a boon when you're pressed for time as they are simple, glamorous and fun.

⌐⌐

antipasti

wild mushroom risotto
with rocket salad

lemon and raspberry iced vodka Martinis
choc-mint Martinis
banoffee Martinis

TO DRINK Italian wines are the instinctive choice with this largely Italian-inspired menu. A dry Italian white such as a Pinot Grigio would go perfectly well with both the antipasto and the risotto. Try one from the Alto Adige in the north-east of Italy, which produces some of the best the country has to offer. Alternatively, you could switch to a supple, medium-bodied Italian red with the main course: something like a Chianti or Rosso di Montepulciano.

antipasti

Make a colourful spread of Italian cured meats and cheeses and roasted or grilled vegetables. Take your pick from Parma ham, two different types of salami (the kind with fennel seeds is particularly delicious), mini mozzarella balls or a buffalo mozzarella and cherry tomato salad (buy some extra fresh basil to garnish), roasted peppers, courgettes and aubergines, grilled artichokes and marinated mushrooms. Serve with ciabatta and breadsticks.

wild mushroom risotto

Risottos always go down well and, once you've got the hang of them, they are incredibly easy to make. Use wild mushrooms in season or chestnut mushrooms with some dried porcini when they're not available.

200 g wild mushrooms or 250 g chestnut mushrooms and 25 g dried porcini, soaked for 15 minutes in warm water

2 tablespoons light olive oil

90 g unsalted butter

1 small–medium onion, finely chopped

300 g arborio or carnaroli risotto rice

1.2 litres homemade chicken stock or stock made with vegetable bouillon powder

125 ml dry white wine

3 heaped tablespoons Parmesan cheese, plus extra to serve

salt and freshly ground black pepper

Serves 4

Clean the fresh mushrooms by lightly brushing or wiping them with a damp cloth. Slice them thinly. If you're using porcini drain them and slice them too. Heat a medium frying pan, add 1 tablespoon of oil and 40 g of the butter and briefly fry the fresh mushrooms until lightly browned. Heat the remaining oil and 25 g of the remaining butter in a large saucepan then add the onion. Stir and cook over a medium heat, for about 3 minutes, then tip in the rice and stir. Let it cook for about 3 minutes without colouring, stirring occasionally so that it doesn't catch on the pan. Meanwhile, heat the stock in another saucepan until it is almost boiling and leave over low heat. Pour the wine into the rice. It will sizzle and evaporate almost immediately. Add the dried mushrooms, if using, then gradually add the stock, a ladleful at a time, stirring the risotto in between and cooking it until the liquid has almost been absorbed. Then add the next lot of stock and repeat until the rice is nice and creamy but still has a little 'bite' to it. This will take about 20 minutes. About 5 minutes before the end of the cooking time, stir in the sautéed mushrooms, leaving a few for garnishing. When the risotto is ready, stir in the remaining butter and Parmesan and season to taste with salt and pepper. Leave the pan covered for a few minutes while you reheat the remaining mushrooms. Serve the risotto in bowls topped with a few mushrooms and some extra Parmesan. Serve with a rocket salad.

Take the sorbets out of the freezer 20 minutes before you want to serve them and transfer to the fridge. Scoop a couple of balls of sorbet into each glass (same flavour or mixed) and pour over a splash of vodka.

* Vodka won't actually freeze but keep it in the freezer and it will be wonderfully cold.

choc-mint Martinis

4 scoops bought chocolate mint ice cream
4 shots chilled or frozen vodka
2 shots coffee-flavoured liqueur, such as Kahlúa
cocoa powder, to garnish

4 Martini glasses, frosted in the freezer

Makes 4 drinks

Put the ice cream in a blender with the vodka and coffee-flavoured liqueur. Whizz until smooth then try the blend, adjusting the proportions of ice cream, vodka or liqueur to taste. Pour into the glasses and sift a little cocoa powder over the surface.

banoffee Martinis

1 ripe banana, sliced
ice cubes
3 shots vanilla-flavoured vodka or ordinary vodka and a few drops of vanilla extract
2 shots toffee- or caramel-flavoured liqueur
2 shots milk
a small pinch of ground nutmeg (optional)
powdered drinking chocolate, to garnish

2 Martini glasses, frosted in the freezer

Makes 2 drinks

Whizz the banana in a blender with the vodka. Tip the purée into a shaker full of ice cubes. Add the toffee liqueur, milk and nutmeg, if using, and shake vigorously. Strain into the glasses and sift a little chocolate powder over the surface.

dessert cocktails

Easy, light, stunning. Iced vodka Martinis are the perfect midweek dessert, so long as you don't have too many of them! Ultra-sweet, creamy cocktails also make a brilliant instant dessert, so try these too.

lemon and raspberry iced vodka Martinis

1 500-ml tub bought lemon sorbet
1 500-ml tub bought raspberry sorbet
1 bottle of frozen* vodka

4 Martini glasses, frosted in the freezer

Makes 4 drinks

a fine wine dinner

menu for 6

Sometimes the starting point for a menu is a bottle – or bottles – of special wine. You may feel you have to pull all the culinary stops out – but don't! Nothing suits fine wines better than simple food. A clean-flavoured seafood starter, a prime cut of meat, an elegant, classic dessert – there's nothing in this meal that's too complicated or that could clash with a treasured bottle. Let the wine be the hero for once...

potted prawns

TO DRINK Potted prawns are an astonishingly good match for good white Burgundy or other mature Chardonnay, so I would kick off with that.

roast fillet of beef with soy and butter sauce

roast new potatoes with garlic and rosemary

TO DRINK The gentle flavours of the meat sauce won't overwhelm an older red wine, so this is the occasion to bring out an aged bottle of Bordeaux, Burgundy, Barolo or a Rioja Gran Reserva that you have been saving for a special occasion.

roast pears with sweet wine, honey and pine nuts

TO DRINK The perfect excuse to crack open a bottle of Sauternes.
Serve it well chilled in small glasses.

chocolates, coffee and cognac

potted prawns

Don't be tempted to use showy tiger prawns for this. The small, sweet ones have much more flavour and suit the dish better.

450 g cooked, shelled North Atlantic prawns, thawed if frozen

200 g unsalted butter, cut into cubes

½ teaspoon ground mace

¼ teaspoon cayenne pepper or hot (piquante) pimentón

a good pinch of sea salt

1 heaped tablespoon finely chopped parsley

a handful of watercress salad, to garnish

wholemeal or Granary toast, to serve

6 ramekins

Serves 6

Drain the prawns thoroughly. Melt the butter very slowly in a medium saucepan. Carefully skim off the milky-looking white layer that will have come to the surface, then mix in the mace and cayenne pepper, adding a little extra to taste if you think it needs it.

Tip the prawns into the butter, mix in well and leave over very low heat for 15 minutes without boiling to allow the flavours to infuse. Take off the heat, add the salt (rub the flakes between your fingers) and stir in the parsley. Spoon the prawns into the ramekins and pour over the remaining melted butter. Press the prawns down firmly with the back of a teaspoon so as much as possible of the prawns are submerged. Cover the dishes with clingfilm and refrigerate for at least a couple of hours – preferably overnight.

Take out of the fridge 15 minutes before serving. Place each ramekin on a small plate and serve with toasted wholemeal or Granary bread.

roast fillet of beef with soy and butter sauce

The soy and butter sauce may sound unconventional, but it makes a very light, savoury, meaty sauce that is much more wine friendly than some of the very intense winey reductions you get in restaurants.

1 teaspoon coarse sea salt
2 teaspoons black peppercorns
½ teaspoon ground allspice
1 tablespoon plain flour
1–1.1 kg flllet of beef
1 tablespoon sunflower or light olive oil
40 g soft butter
2 tablespoons Madeira or dry Marsala
375 ml fresh beef stock or stock made with ¾ organic, low-salt beef stock cube
1½ tablespoons Japanese soy sauce, such as Kikkoman

a cast-iron casserole or deep roasting tin

Serves 6

Preheat the oven to 225°C (425°F) Gas 7. Put the coarse salt and peppercorns in a mortar and grind with a pestle until finely ground. Mix in the allspice and flour. Remove any fat or sinew from the beef fillet and dry thoroughly with kitchen paper. Put the seasoning and flour on a plate and roll the beef in the mixture, patting it evenly into the surface and shaking off any excess. Put the casserole or roasting tin over medium to high heat, add the oil and half the butter and brown the beef quickly on all sides. Transfer to the preheated oven and roast for 20–40 minutes, depending how thick your beef fillet is and how rare you like it. Remove from the oven and set aside for 10–15 minutes, lightly covered with foil. Pour off any excess fat in the pan, leaving about 1 tablespoon. Pour in the Madeira and let it bubble up for a few seconds, then add the stock and soy sauce. Bring to the boil, turn the heat down a little

and reduce by half. Pour any juices that have accumulated under the meat into the pan, whisk in the remaining butter and season with black pepper (you shouldn't need any salt).

Carve the meat into thick slices and serve on warmed plates with the sauce spooned over and served with some roast new potatoes (see below) and green beans.

roast new potatoes with garlic and rosemary

1 kg even-sized small new potatoes
1 litre vegetable stock made with organic vegetable stock cube or 4 teaspoons vegetable bouillon powder
2 tablespoons olive oil
3 garlic cloves, unpeeled
2–3 sprigs of rosemary
sea salt flakes

a roasting dish

Serves 6

Preheat the oven to 220°C (425°F) Gas 7. Scrub the potatoes well and put in a saucepan. Cover with the boiling vegetable stock, bring back to the boil and cook for about 5–6 minutes. Drain well and tip into a roasting dish. Pour over the olive oil and toss the potatoes so that they are evenly coated. Crush the garlic cloves lightly, distribute them around the dish, together with the sprigs of rosemary. Toss again and roast in the preheated oven for about 20–25 minutes until nicely browned, turning the potatoes halfway through. Discard the garlic and rosemary, sprinkle the potatoes with salt flakes and serve.

roast pears with sweet wine, honey and pine nuts

Roasting pears in wine transforms them from everyday fruit into a light but luxurious dessert. The trick is to use an inexpensive wine for cooking and a better wine of the same type to serve with it.

freshly squeezed juice of 1 lemon (about 3 tablespoons)

9 just-ripe, small Conference pears

50 g butter, softened

3 tablespoons fragrant honey

175 ml Premières Côtes de Bordeaux or late-harvested Sauvignon or Semillon

50 g pine nuts

1 dessertspoon unrefined caster sugar

200 ml double cream

2 teaspoons vanilla sugar or ½ teaspoon vanilla extract and 2 teaspoons caster sugar

a large roasting tin or ovenproof dish (big enough to take the pears in a single layer), well buttered

Serves 6

Preheat the oven to 190°C (375°F) Gas 5. Strain the lemon juice into a small bowl. Cut each pear in half, peel it and cut away the core. Dip it in the lemon juice to stop it discolouring. Place it cut-side upwards in the roasting tin or dish. Arrange the pears so that they fit snugly in one layer. Put a knob of butter in the centre of each half. Drizzle the pears with the honey and pour over the leftover lemon juice and the wine.

Bake in the preheated oven for about 50 minutes –1 hour, turning the pears halfway through. If the pears produce a lot of juice turn the heat up to 200°C (400°F) Gas 6 to concentrate the juices and form a syrup.

Remove from the oven and let cool for about 20 minutes. (You can part-cook the dish for about 30 minutes a couple of hours before dinner, then finish cooking it once you sit down at table, allowing it to cool during the main course.)

Meanwhile, toast the pine nuts lightly in a frying pan, shaking them occasionally until they start to brown. Sprinkle over the caster sugar and continue to cook until the sugar melts and caramelizes. Sweeten the cream with the vanilla sugar and heat until lukewarm. Arrange 3 pear halves on each plate, trickle over about a tablespoon of warm cream and scatter over the pine nuts.

chocolates, coffee and cognac

For a special occasion, you can serve this at the
end of the meal, otherwise it makes a great
substitute for a dessert. Source the best hand-made
chocolates you can find, preferably made from dark
chocolate, including some truffles for contrast.
Brew up some real coffee – espresso for those who
want it and an Americano for those who prefer
a less intense brew – and serve with the best
cognac or Spanish brandy you can afford.

seasonal cheeseboards

Wine and cheese is supposed to be the perfect match, but how often have you been disappointed at the combination? Your favourite red wine may taste great with one or two of the cheeses on the board, but clash horribly with another. Or a delicate cheese may be totally overwhelmed by the wine. It's time we changed the way we think about cheeseboards, designing them, like other foods we serve, to reflect the seasons and our mood. It's an approach that makes abundant sense, as so many cheeses themselves are seasonal. Why serve the same cheeseboard in June as you do in December?

It also helps to limit the number of cheeses you serve and pick them carefully. If you include a strong, stinky French cheese and a pungent blue in your selection, for example, you'll struggle to find a wine to go with them both. The traditional approach is to serve the widest range of cheeses you can afford, displaying your generosity as a host, but the chances are that your guests will enjoy the experience just as much if you select two or three that work perfectly together.

You can also be a bit more imaginative about the way you dress your cheeseboard, introducing accompaniments that will complement the flavour of your cheeses and reflect the time of year. Warm, rich dried fruits, for example, in winter when fresh fruits are less widely available; fresh salad leaves in spring. Finally, don't get too struck on the idea that the only accompaniment for a cheeseboard is a glass of red wine. There are many other drinks that work just as well. Crisp white wines in spring, for example, or a glass of sweet sherry or Madeira rather than port. It's sometimes a great deal easier to find a Belgian beer to match a powerful cheese than a wine and artisanal cider can also be a great pairing.

spring

Spring and early summer is the ideal time of year to enjoy fresh young goats' cheeses and their perfect partner Sauvignon Blanc. Choose two or three cheeses for contrast: one young, light and moussey, one that has been matured a little longer and one that has been rolled in herbs. Serve them with a lightly dressed herb salad bought from the farmers' market. You could also add a wedge of tangy, fresh Italian pecorino and a few shelled broad beans, a delicious combination. Breads should be light too – slices of ciabatta and some crisp Italian flatbread such as *carta di musica*. My preferred choice of Sauvignon would be a minerally Sancerre or Pouilly Fumé, but choose any unoaked Sauvignon that you enjoy.

summer

Now the flavours are richer and fuller, begging for a full-bodied red wine. The type of cheese that works best are the smooth, tangy hard sheeps' cheeses you traditionally find in Spain and the Basque region of France, full flavoured but without any touch of bitterness. I also like to add a Fleur de Maquis, a Corsican cheese rolled in rosemary and fennel. Add some other Mediterranean ingredients – a few chewy sun-dried tomatoes, some olives and olive bread – and you've got the perfect foil for a rich southern French red from the Languedoc or the Rhône, or a Spanish red like a Rioja.

autumn

The ploughman's lunch re-invented. Forget wine for once and turn to cider, the natural accompaniment for autumn fruits and flavours. Mix and match among ancient and modern British and Irish cheeses – a fine Cheddar, an Irish Adrahan or other washed-rind cheese, a snowy white-rinded Tunworth, maybe even a mellow blue. Serve with fine, flavourful eating apples and pears, a mild apple chutney (homemade or bought) and an old-fashioned white crusty loaf, and pour chunky glasses of cool, artisanal cider, offering your guests a choice of dry or medium-dry if you wish. You could even offer brandy glasses of Somerset Cider Brandy or Calvados to round off the meal.

winter

Port and blue cheese is a classic pairing, but give it a modern twist. Serve three contrasting cheeses, say a Stilton, a Roquefort and a mild Gorgonzola or Harbourne Blue (a mild blue goats' cheese from Devon) and serve them with a top class collection of dried fruits such as Medjool dates, figs or raisins and a handful of walnuts and brazil nuts. Echo the dried fruit flavours with my simple raisin and rosemary bread or a walnut bread, and introduce a little crunch with a few handcut oat biscuits or oatcakes. This is the perfect occasion to bring out a vintage port (which you'll need to decant) or serve a fine Sauternes or a Tokay from Hungary. What blue cheeses need is sweetness.

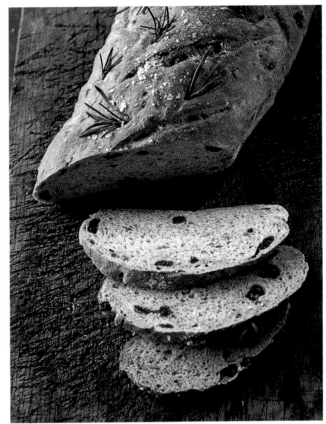

Vivid orange Mimolette served with Medjool dates, dried apricots and figs makes a perfect winter cheese plate. Serve with a hearty red such as a Syrah or Shiraz.

raisin and rosemary bread

A quick, simple bread that's perfect for cheese.

250 g strong white flour

150 g strong wholemeal flour

100 g rye flour

1½ teaspoons easy-blend or quick-acting yeast

1½ teaspoons fine sea salt

1 tablespoon finely chopped rosemary, plus 2 extra sprigs for topping

1 tablespoon soft dark brown sugar

310 ml tepid water

2 tablespoons olive oil

110 g raisins

a baking tray, lightly oiled

Makes 1 large loaf

Mix together the white, wholemeal and rye flours in a large bowl. Mix in the yeast, salt and chopped rosemary. Dissolve the sugar in 2 tablespoons of the water. Make a well in the middle of the flour and pour in the dissolved sugar and olive oil, followed by the rest of the water. Start working the flour into the liquid with a wooden spoon, then mix with your hands until all the flour is incorporated. Turn the dough onto a floured board and knead for 5 minutes or until the dough begins to feel elastic. Flatten the dough and add half the raisins. Fold over and knead for a couple of seconds, then repeat with the remaining raisins. Carry on kneading for another 5 minutes until smooth. Place the dough in a large bowl covered with a lightly dampened tea towel and leave for about 45–50 minutes until doubled in size. Tip the dough out of the bowl and press down on it to knock out the air. Roll up the dough into a long sausage shape, tucking in the ends. Place on the baking tray, make 3–4 diagonal cuts in the dough with a sharp knife, cover with the tea towel and leave for another 25 minutes. Meanwhile, heat the oven to 200°C (400°F) Gas 6. Brush the top of the loaf lightly with water and scatter over the leaves from the rosemary sprigs, pressing them lightly into the dough. Bake for about 35–40 minutes until the loaf is well browned and sounds hollow when you tap it on the base. Cool on a wire rack for a good 45 minutes before serving.

just desserts

An alternative to inviting people round for a meal or drinks and nibbles, is to just invite them round for something sweet. It could be simply to join you for dessert, or for a nightcap and a sweet nibble. Or you could host an old-fashioned coffee morning (see page 142) – whatever happened to that tradition? Or why not host an indulgent Chocolate Evening – see page 145 for plenty of ideas. There are so many ways to play this...

You could offer a selection of petit fours or dessert tapas (see page 71) – little cakes and tartlets, colourful macaroons or meringues, homemade mini florentines (opposite), served with some different sweet wines to try. I find liqueurs are frequently better than wines with chocolate desserts. Think of the flavours you find in a box of liqueur chocolates – cherry, apricot, orange, blackcurrant, mint, coffee, hazelnut, almond and you can find an equivalent liqueur (cherry or apricot brandy, Grand Marnier, cassis, crème de menthe, Kahlùa, Frangelico and Disaronno, for example). Most taste best lightly chilled; some, like cherry brandy, are good frozen. Serve them in shot glasses or antique liqueur glasses and your friends will be truly impressed.

cranberry and cherry florentines

These have to be the easiest biscuits in the world, but they look sensationally impressive.

100 g butter
100 g unrefined caster sugar
1 dessertspoon fragrant clear honey
75 g blanched almonds
110 g mixed sun-dried cranberries, cherries and blueberries
100 g plain flour
125 g good-quality dark chocolate (minimum 70% cocoa solids)
2–3 non-stick baking trays or baking trays lined with non-stick baking parchment

Makes 20–24 biscuits

Preheat the oven to 180°C (350°F) Gas 4. Put the butter, sugar and honey in a saucepan and melt over low heat. When the sugar has dissolved, bring almost to boiling point, then take the pan off the hob. Stir in the almonds and fruit, then tip in the flour and mix thoroughly. Spoon heaped teaspoonfuls of the mixture onto the baking sheets, leaving plenty of space between each blob. Flatten them slightly with the back of your spoon so that they cook evenly and bake for 10–12 minutes until the florentines have spread and are turning brown at the edges. Take them out of the oven, cool for about 3 minutes, then carefully prise them off the baking trays and transfer them to a wire rack. When they are completely cold, break the chocolate into squares, place it in a heatproof bowl and melt in the microwave or over a pan of barely simmering water, taking care that the bowl doesn't touch the water. Lay the biscuits flat-side upwards on a sheet of greaseproof paper and brush or spread the chocolate over them with a pastry brush or a flat-bladed knife. Leave them out until the chocolate sets, then store in an airtight tin.

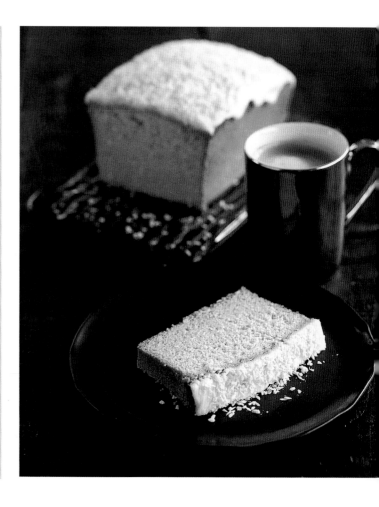

Malibu, lime and coconut cake

Even if you're not a fan of Malibu, I promise you you'll love this exotic coconut-flavoured cake. If you are, you'll be in seventh heaven!

175 g unsalted butter, at room temperature, diced

150 g unrefined caster sugar

3 large eggs

200 g self-raising flour

25 g coconut milk powder

½ teaspoon baking powder

3 tablespoons Malibu (coconut-flavoured liqueur)

a little grated lime zest

125 g icing sugar, sifted twice

1–1½ tablespoons freshly squeezed lime juice

25 g toasted or dessicated coconut

a lightly greased 900-g loaf tin lined with a strip of baking parchment

Serves 8–10

Preheat the oven to 160°C (325°F) Gas 3. Put the butter in a large bowl with the sugar and beat with an electric hand-held whisk or a wooden spoon until light and fluffy. Lightly beat one of the eggs and add it to the mixture with a tablespoon of the flour that has been sifted along with the coconut milk powder and baking powder. Beat in well and repeat with the remaining eggs, adding a spoonful of flour with each addition. Mix in the Malibu, then add the remaining flour and coconut powder, mixing in lightly and quickly. Spoon into the prepared loaf tin and spread the top evenly. Bake in the preheated oven for 45–50 minutes until the cake is well risen and firm and slightly shrunken away from the sides. Remove the tin from the oven and cool for 10 minutes, then turn the cake out of the tin and leave to cool on a wire rack. Mix the lime zest with the sifted icing sugar and add just enough lime juice to make a thick but still spreadable consistency. Spread or pour over the top of the cake and sprinkle over the toasted coconut.

This is delicious served with a good French-style café crème, a white coffee with a little bit of froth, but not as frothy as an Italian cappuccino.

sticky toffee pudding cake

150 g dried dates, chopped

1 teaspoon bicarbonate of soda

225 ml moderately strong hot black coffee (e.g. from a cafétière)

150 g plain flour

50 g butter, chilled and cut into cubes

50 g walnuts, finely chopped

200 g golden caster sugar

1 teaspoon baking powder

½ teaspoon fine sea salt

½ teaspoon vanilla extract

1 large egg

For the topping:

50 g walnuts, finely chopped

1 teaspoon golden caster sugar

25 g unsalted butter

4 tablespoons soft light brown sugar

4 tablespoons whipping cream

a rectangular, non-stick baking tin 30.5 x 20.5 cm, lightly greased

Makes 15 squares

Preheat the oven to 180°C (350°F) Gas 4. Put the chopped dates in a bowl, add the bicarbonate of soda and pour over the hot coffee. Put the flour in another bowl, tip in the cubed butter and cut and rub it in until it resembles coarse breadcrumbs.

Add the chopped walnuts to the flour mixture with the sugar, baking powder and salt. Beat the egg with the vanilla extract and add to the date mixture then tip the date mixture, into the dry ingredients and beat well. Turn the mixture into the prepared baking tin. Bake in the preheated oven for about 35–40 minutes or until well risen and firm to the touch. Remove from the oven and let cool for 10 minutes while you make the topping.

Heat the walnuts in a saucepan with the caster sugar, shaking them occasionally until they are lightly toasted. Combine the butter in a small saucepan with the brown sugar and cream. Heat over low heat, stirring until the sugar has dissolved, then bring to the boil. Pour evenly over the cake, smoothing over the icing with a knife, then scatter the toasted walnuts on top. When the cake is completely cool, cut it into squares and carefully remove from the tin using a cake slice or palate knife.

This is particularly good served with freshly brewed black coffee.

No-one – even if they're on a diet – is going to refuse an invitation to come round for a chocolate evening (if they hesitate, just tell them they don't need to eat the next day...). There are so many ways to play it. You could serve a variety of different chocolate desserts such as some individual mousses or chocolate pots, a chocolate cake and a chocolate tart such as the one opposite, one of my all-time favourite recipes.

Alternatively, you could serve a selection of different chocolate cakes and biscuits – some chocolate muffins and warm chocolate chip cookies. You could even have friends round for an indulgent chocolate fondue, offering fruits such as strawberries, apricots and pieces of banana for dunking into the molten chocolate.

You could base the event – although this would be more of a morning than an evening occasion – on hot drinking chocolate and serve baskets of Danish pastries or some French pâtisserie, such as pain au chocolat. Or just keep it simple and invite friends round for chocolate and cognac after dinner (see page 135).

If your event is a success you could start a local chocolate club, meeting with friends once a month for different chocolate-themed evenings and trying new chocolate recipes from around the world?

hazelnut, chocolate and cardamom cream pie

For the pastry:
60 g unsalted butter, softened
25 g icing sugar
100 g hazelnuts
125 g plain flour, unsifted
1 egg yolk

For the filling:
10 green cardamoms
300 ml double cream
200 g good-quality dark chocolate (minimum 70% cocoa solids), broken into chunks
25 g unsalted butter
1 tablespoon cocoa powder, sifted, to decorate

a baking tray
a 23-cm fluted flan tin

Serves 8

Preheat the oven to 190°C (375°F) Gas 5. Spread the hazelnuts out on a baking tray and toast in the preheated oven for 15 minutes or until lightly browned. Cool, then chop in a food processor or coffee grinder (you may have to do this in batches). Cream the butter with the sifted icing sugar, add 40 g of the hazelnuts then gradually work in the flour. Beat the egg yolk with 1 tablespoon water and add to the mixture, gradually pulling it into a ball.

Turn out onto a floured board or work surface and roll or press it out gently into a round slightly smaller than the flan tin. Carefully lower it into the tin (don't worry if it breaks) and press it round and up the side until you have formed a pastry case. Chill in the fridge for at least half an hour, then prick the base and bake it in the oven for about 15–20 minutes until lightly browned. Let cool.

Meanwhile, crush the cardamoms with in a mortar with a pestle or with the end of a rolling pin. Remove the green husks and finely grind the seeds. Add to the cream and gently warm in a saucepan until the surface is just beginning to tremble. (Don't let it boil). Take off the heat and add the chocolate chunks, butter and the remaining ground hazelnuts. Set aside to cool, but don't let it get cold. Pour into the pastry case and put in the fridge for at least 2 hours. Dust the surface with cocoa powder before serving.

This is delicious with a glass of Frangelico (hazelnut liqueur).

the art of party planning

It's easy to lose sight of the main reason for having a party: to enjoy yourself and to make sure your guests have a good time. All too often your worries about what food to serve and whether your guests will get on becomes such an overriding concern or you spend so much time slaving away in the kitchen that you end up completely stressed and worn out. The good news, though, is that it's never been easier to throw a party without spending hours cooking or spending a fortune on caterers. You can literally buy in everything you need – canapés, platters of cold meats or seafood, hot dishes, vegetables, salads, cheeseboards and gorgeous, gooey desserts – which completely takes the terror out of entertaining. If you tell yourself that you don't have to cook a thing if you don't want to, you can then concentrate on the dishes you do best or most enjoy making. What you do need to do is to focus on what sort of party you want, so ask yourself the following questions:

WHAT SORT OF PARTY IS IT?

Do you want to celebrate something special or simply to get a few friends together? Do you want it to be an occasion that everyone will remember or just a relaxed affair? Are you happy for it to last for hours or do you just want to 'pay your dues' with a pop-in-when-you-like drinks party for neighbours or colleagues at work?

CAN YOU PULL IT OFF?

Have you got the space to invite as many people as you want? Or the equipment (see page 148)? Can you throw the sort of party you have in mind on your budget? Do you have the time – or the skill – to prepare the sort of meal you're planning? For example, if you've never cooked for more than four friends before, you might find cooking for 20 daunting without help. If so, how are you going to get round that? Get professional help? Buy in ready-made dishes? Enlist help from family and friends? If you're going to make part of the food yourself, don't leave yourself too many things that require last-minute attention or embark on recipes that you've never attempted before.

THE MENU

There are plenty of menus in the book that can be adapted for a crowd – just remember when you're scaling up recipes for larger numbers that not every ingredient needs to be doubled or trebled. Go easy on spices and other seasonings, tasting before you add more.

Quantities will vary depending on the age and sex of your guests (younger guests and men tending to eat more than older guests and women), but as a general rule I would allow six to eight canapés or nibbles per person for a drinks party, of which one or two could be sweet, and one and a half servings in total of any main course, two servings of salad or vegetables and two of dessert, on the assumption that a third to a half of your guests will come back for a second helping. If you want to limit the amount that your guests eat, don't offer too many options, as people like to try everything, especially desserts!

Remember to check if there is anything your guests can't eat. Food intolerances are quite common these days, so it's wise to have at least one option that is vegetarian, wheat- and dairy-free (rice-based dishes are particularly useful in this respect).

THE DRINK

Again, the more different types of drink you offer, the more your guests will drink and the more glasses they'll use. A choice of two types of wine, two different soft drinks and water is plenty, although you can obviously lay on one or two beers and jug drinks (much easier than making individual cocktails) if you wish.

A reasonable amount to cater for is half a bottle of wine per head, although if a party is due to go on for quite a time or you have guests who are likely to drink rather more than that, allow a bottle each in total.

Good choices for a drinks party are Champagne or sparkling wine or a light, refreshing white and a soft, fruity red. (Avoid wines that are heavily oaked or high in alcohol, which can easily result in your guests drinking more than they realize and can also make them uncomfortably hot and flushed.) As a general rule, you'll probably need twice as much white wine as red.

For an event with hot food, you need wines with a little more weight – consult my food and wine matching guidelines overleaf for the individual dishes you're planning to serve. Either way, it's best to go for wines that everyone will enjoy and that are not too hard on the pocket. When I'm catering for large numbers, I tend to go for easy crowd-pleasers rather than more esoteric wines – lighter styles of Chardonnay and Sauvignon Blanc for the whites and soft reads such as Merlot or Pinot Noir for the reds. If you're holding an outdoor event like a barbecue, you could easily serve rosé instead of a white, so popular has it become. Pink fizz is also great fun too, especially for a summer tea party (see page 56).

Finally, avoid the temptation to buy a job lot of cheap wine that you haven't tried before just because it's on special offer. Often stores discount wines that have reached the end of their shelf-life, so you may end up with a batch that's tasting rather flat and tired. If at all possible, try a bottle before you buy the case.

THE EQUIPMENT

It's rare to have enough glasses, plates and cutlery to cater for a crowd, so make sure you hire or borrow enough for everyone. Many wine shops and supermarkets now offer glass hire – play safe and allow two wine glasses per head.

You also need plenty of ice and large buckets or bins to keep wine and beer cool. (Water and ice used together is more effective than ice alone.)

If you're organizing a barbecue or any other event that requires special equipment (such as blenders or juicers for a juice bar – see page 19), again, make sure you have a sufficient number to avoid long delays in producing the food or drinks.

matching wine to food

Finding a precise match for a dish can be tricky because there are so many variables: how it is cooked, whether there are any strong spice or herbal accents, how many other ingredients there are on the plate. So, to make it as easy as possible, I've concentrated on the style of food here rather than individual dishes, but giving specific examples where appropriate. If you don't find what you're looking for here, do look it up on my website: www.matchingfoodandwine.com

SOUPS

You don't always need wine with a soup, as one liquid doesn't really need another. The thicker the soup, the easier it is to match.

Thin soups e.g. consommés, spicy South-East Asian broths are better without wine, although dry sherry will go with a traditional consommé.

Smooth creamy soups e.g. light vegetable soups: go for a smooth, dry, unoaked white such as Chablis or Soave.

Chunky soups should be treated as you would a stew – they can take a medium-bodied white or a red wine such as a Côtes du Rhône.

STARTERS

Given that they're served at the beginning of a meal, a crisp, dry white, aromatic white or rosé is generally most appropriate. Sometimes a light red can work too.

Cold, fish-based starters such as prawn or crab salads or terrines: a crisp, dry white such as Sancerre or other Loire Sauvignon Blanc, or a Riesling (particularly good with smoked fish). Chablis is the classic match for oysters.

Hot, fish-based starters e.g fishcakes or scallops: Chardonnay is usually a safe bet except with spicy flavours when unoaked, fruity or aromatic whites work better.

Charcuterie (saucisson, salami, pâtés and air-dried hams): dry rosé and light reds like Beaujolais.

Meat-based salads made with duck or with chicken livers: Pinot Noir.

Cheese-based starters with salads and cold quiches try unoaked Chardonnay, while goats' cheese works well with Sauvignon Blanc. Champagne or sparkling wine pairs well with deep-fried cheese starters.

Vegetable-based starters e.g. terrines: follow similar recommendations to cold fish-based starters opposite. (Asparagus works well with Sauvignon Blanc.)

Tapas: chilled fino or manzanilla sherry (see page 66).

PASTA, PIZZA AND NOODLES

It's not the type of pasta you use that determines your choice of wine, it's the sauce you put with it.

Creamy sauces e.g. spaghetti carbonara: smooth, dry, Italian unoaked whites such as Soave and Pinot Bianco.

Seafood-based sauces: crisp, dry Italian whites and citrussy Sauvignon Blancs.

Tomato-based sauces: fresh tomato sauces – crisp, dry whites such as Pinot Grigio or Sauvignon Blanc: cooked tomato sauces – a light Italian red such as Chianti or a Barbera.

Cheese-based sauces: crisp, dry, intensely flavoured whites – good Pinot Grigio or a modern Sardinian white.

Rich meat or aubergine-based sauces e.g. Bolognese: a fruity Italian red such as a Barbera or a Sangiovese, or a southern Italian or Sicilian red.

Baked pasta dishes e.g. meat lasagne: a good Chianti.

Pizza: generally, I think fruity Italian reds work better than whites, except with seafood pizzas.

Noodles: generally spicy, so crisp fruity whites or aromatic whites such as Riesling tend to work best.

RICE

Rice dishes work in a similar way to pasta with wine.

Risotto: Most light vegetable- and seafood-based risottos pair well with crisp, dry whites such as good-quality Pinot Grigio or Soave and with sparkling wines like Champagne. Richer risottos based on dried mushrooms (porcini) or beetroot can take a red (Pinot Noir and Dolcetto respectively).

Spicy rice (e.g. paella, jambalaya): dry southern French or Spanish rosé and tempranillo-based reds such as those from Rioja and Navarra.

Sushi: Muscadet or dry Champagne, especially Blanc de Blancs.

FISH

Cooked simply, fish is quite delicate, but more robust cooking techniques and saucing can call for more powerful wines.

Raw fish e.g. sushi, sashimi: see notes for Sushi, above.

Pickled fish e.g. herring: lager, especially pilsener, works better than wine.

Oily fish e.g. mackerel, sardines: sharp, lemony whites such as Rueda and modern Greek whites.

Smoked fish: dry Riesling or Spanish manzanilla sherry.

Salmon: served cold – unoaked Chardonnay e.g. Chablis; served hot in a pie or with pastry – lightly-oaked Chardonnay; with a hot butter sauce – a richer Chardonnay; seared or marinated with a spicy crust – a light red such as Pinot Noir.

Tuna: served cold in salad – Sauvignon Blanc or dry rosé; seared or barbecued, a chilled Pinot Noir.

Fish in a creamy sauce including fish pie: lightly oaked Chardonnay, Chenin Blanc or oaked white Bordeaux.

Pan-fried or grilled fish: If simply prepared this is an occasion to drink good white Burgundy or other top-quality Chardonnay or a clean-flavoured white like Albariño.

Fish and chips and other fried fish: crisp, dry whites such as Sauvignon Blanc or a sparkling wine.

Seared, roasted or barbecued fish: can often take a light red, such as Pinot Noir, especially if wrapped in pancetta or served with lentils or beans.

BIRDS AND GAME

Chicken

Being a neutrally flavoured bird, you need to focus more on the way chicken is cooked and the sauce that accompanies it than the chicken itself (see page 9–11). See also recommendations for pasta sauces (opposite) and spicy food (page 152).

Roast chicken: Good white or red Burgundy or quality New World Chardonnay or Pinot Noir; softer, riper styles of Bordeaux e.g. Pomerol and Merlot.

Grilled or chargrilled chicken: Will depend on the baste or the marinade – lighter, citrussy, herbal flavours suggest a crisp, fruity white like a Sauvignon Blanc; a spicier, sweeter marinade would work better with a jammy red like a Shiraz.

With tomatoes, peppers and olives: a fruity, Italian red or other Sangiovese.

Coq au vin and other red wine sauces: a similar red wine to the one you use to make the dish (a robust Rhône or Languedoc red or a Syrah, I suggest).

Fried chicken: unoaked or lightly oaked Chardonnay.

Sweet and sour or fruity sauces: Fruity Australian whites such as Semillon, Semillon-Chardonnay or Colombard, or ripe, fruity reds such as Merlot.

Chicken salads: depends a bit on the dressing. An unoaked Chardonnay or a fruity rosé will cover most eventualities but if there's a South-East Asian twist to the recipe, a Sauvignon Blanc, Riesling, Verdelho or Viognier is likely to work much better.

Turkey

See chicken, but bear in mind that on festive occasions a roast turkey is likely to be accompanied by a flavoursome stuffing, fruity cranberry sauce and richly flavoured vegetables such as parsnips and butternut squash, which call for a more full-bodied red than a plain roast chicken: something like a fruity Pinot Noir, Shiraz or even Châteauneuf-du-Pape.

Duck

Pinot Noir almost always works except with duck confit, which is better with darker, more full-bodied southern French or Spanish red.

MEAT

Pork

Very similar in flavour to chicken, but the extra fattiness calls for wines with a little more acidity. *See also the sauces listed under Chicken, Pasta and Spicy Food.*

Roast pork: If flavoured Italian-style with garlic and fennel, choose a dry Italian white. Otherwise try a soft, fruity red such as a Pinot Noir, Merlot or a good cru Beaujolais. Chenin Blanc and Riesling are good with cold roast pork.

Pork with apples and cider: cider is better than wine.

Sausages: robust, fruity southern French or Spanish red.

Hot gammon: a fruity red such as Merlot or a Carmenère.

Cold ham: Chablis or other unoaked Chardonnay and Beaujolais.

See also Charcuterie under Starters.

Lamb

Roast or grilled lamb: a good partner for a serious red, particularly red Bordeaux and other Cabernet- and Merlot-based wines, Rioja and Chianti Classico.

Lamb shanks and casseroles: robust, rustic reds such as those from the Rhône, Southern France and Spain.

Greek-style lamb kebabs with mint and lemon: can be partnered with a fruity red but equally good with a citrussy white.

Lamb tagines: Rioja Reserva or soft, pruney southern Italian reds. *See also Spicy Foods.*

Beef and venison

Roasts and steaks: any fine red you enjoy. Argentinian Malbec is a particularly good steak wine.

Casseroles, stews and pies: can cover quite a wide range of flavours from a beef stew with dumplings (for which beer is a better accompaniment than wine) to a rich oxtail stew (try Zinfandel). A useful guide is that if you use wine to make the stew, drink a robust red; if you use beer, drink ale.

Teriyaki or stir-fried beef: a ripe fruity red such as a Chilean or Australian Cabernet Sauvignon or a full-bodied New World Pinot Noir. *See also Spicy Foods.*

Veal

For many dishes my recommendations would be similar to those for pork although given the cost of veal, you might feel justified in indulging in a rather better bottle of wine!

Veal escalopes: dry Italian whites such as Pinot Grigio or an Italian red like Chianti.

Osso buco: Italian dry whites such as Soave just have the edge on reds, I feel.

VEGETABLES

Vegetables are no different from any other ingredient – you need to think about the way they're cooked when you're debating what to drink. They are, however, more seasonal than other foods, so the time of year may affect your wine choice.

Spring vegetables and salads e.g. asparagus, peas and broad beans: crisp fresh, fruity whites such as Sauvignon Blanc and Grüner Veltliner.

Summer vegetables e.g. Mediterranean vegetables such as tomatoes, peppers, aubergines and courgettes: dry rosés and medium-bodied southern French and Italian reds.

Autumn vegetables e.g. sweetcorn, squash, pumpkin and mushrooms: a buttery Chardonnay goes particularly well with the first three. A lighter Chardonnay or Pinot Noir are both good choices with mushrooms.

Winter vegetables e.g. onions, carrots, parsnips and dark leafy greens: often served in hearty dishes such as stews and soups, which tend to suit rustic reds and ales.

Vegetarian dishes: vegetarian bakes that contain beans or cheese again suit hearty

reds, but you will need to check that they are suitable for vegetarians (i.e. that no animal-derived products have been used in making them).

CHEESE

Red wine isn't always the best choice with cheese, as I explain on pages 136–138.

Goats' cheese: Sauvignon Blanc and English dry whites.

Camembert and Brie-style cheeses: fruity reds such as Pinot Noir and Merlot. Cider is particularly good with Camembert.

Cheddar and other hard cheeses: aged Spanish reds such as Rioja.

Strong washed-rind cheeses such as Epoisses and Munster: strong Belgian beers work better than wine, although Gewürztraminer is a classic pairing for Munster.

Blue Cheeses: sweet wines, port or sweeter sherries.

Hot cheese dishes: white wines generally work better than reds, unless it's a baked pasta dish like lasagne. With a fondue you need a really crisp, dry white like a Chasselas from Switzerland. With a macaroni cheese, try a light Chardonnay.

DESSERTS

You may not always want to serve a dessert wine, but there are some luscious pairings to experience.

Apple, pear, peach and apricot-based desserts: simple French-style fruit tarts are the perfect foil for a great dessert wine like Sauternes. Apricot tarts work well with sweet Muscat.

Strawberry and raspberry desserts: need light, lemony dessert wines with good acidity like late-harvest Sauvignon and Riesling. Strawberries can be macerated in a light, fruity red wine such as Beaujolais.

Lemon-flavoured desserts: can be tricky,

especially if intensely lemony. Very sweet German and Austrian dessert wines tend to work best. Serving cream with them helps.

Light, creamy desserts e.g. gâteaux and pavlovas: demi-sec Champagne or Moscato d'Asti.

Toffee- or caramel-flavoured desserts e.g. tarte tatin, pecan pie: late-harvested and liqueur Muscats work well with these.

Chocolate desserts: sweet reds are often easier to match than sweet whites – see page 94 and page 145.

SPICY FOOD

Spice is not the enemy of wine that it's reputed to be so long as you avoid wines that are very tannic. It's only really hot chillies that cause a problem.

Mildly spiced dishes including Middle-Eastern mezze, grills and mild Indian curries: simple, crisp fruity whites and dry rosés work best. *See also Lamb Tagines.*

Moderately hot curries such as Rogan Josh: Inexpensive fruity New World reds such as Cabernet-Shiraz blends. With chicken curries try a Semillon-Chardonnay.

Hot curries: Tricky but try Gewürztraminer or Pinotage. Otherwise stick to lager or the Indian yoghurt-based drink, lassi.

Smoked chilli, paprika or pimentón-based dishes such as Chilli con Carne, Goulash or bean dishes flavoured with chorizo: Soft, fruity reds such as Rioja, other aged Spanish reds and Zinfandel.

Thai salads and curries: better with whites than reds. Alsace Riesling and Tokay Pinot Gris work well, as does Gewürztraminer especially with red Thai curries.

matching food to wine

Sometimes the starting point for a meal is not a menu but a wine: a treasured bottle that you've been looking for an occasion to drink, a gift that you want to share with the donor or simply a serendipitous find that inspires you into the kitchen. Of course, you can enjoy it with many of the recipes in this book, particularly those in the Fine Wine Dinner (see page 130), but here are some lists of ingredients and dishes that will flatter good wines:

WHITES

Chardonnay: Lighter styles such as Chablis and good white Burgundy are perfect for simply prepared grilled fish such as plaice, dover sole or salmon, or delicate shellfish like scallops or prawns. Richer Chardonnays are fabulous with roast or sautéed chicken or veal, especially with wild mushrooms, with creamy or buttery sauces or with rich-tasting autumnal vegetables like squash and pumpkin.

Sauvignon Blanc: Unoaked Sauvignon is perfect for healthy, fresh-tasting fish dishes such as grilled seabass, spring vegetables, especially asparagus, and goats' cheese. Oaked Sauvignons, especially those that are blended with Semillon as in Bordeaux, work with similar dishes to Chardonnay.

Riesling: Dry rieslings are shown off best by delicate seafood like fresh crab, prawns and lightly smoked fish such as trout or salmon. Slightly sweeter styles are good with duck, goose and subtly spiced fusion dishes with Asian influences.

Pinot Grigio/Pinot Gris: Like other dry Italian whites, Pinot Grigio is a good choice for antipasti and seafood-based pasta or risotto and simply grilled fish. Richer Pinot Gris, which often has a note of sweetness, works better with lightly spiced chicken and pork dishes, especially if given a South-East Asian twist.

Viognier: Works with similar dishes to Chardonnay, especially chicken, but can handle a little more spice.

Gewürztraminer: This exotically scented white isn't to everyone's taste, but it comes into its own with spicy food, especially Thai and moderately spiced Indian curries. It's also good with duck.

REDS

Pinot Noir e.g. red Burgundy: Duck is almost always a great choice with young fruity Pinot Noir as is simply roasted chicken and turkey and seared tuna. Older Pinots are good with guinea fowl and game birds such as pheasant and partridge.

Cabernet Sauvignon, Merlot and blends of the two e.g. red Bordeaux: You can't go wrong with roast beef or lamb, a good steak or some simply grilled lamb chops. If you're dealing with an older vintage, keep any accompanying sauce and vegetables light – the natural meat juices are the best accompaniment.

Syrah/shiraz: French Syrahs such as those from the Northern Rhône are again good with red meat, but can take more robust treatment – intensely flavoured winey stews, for example, or meat that's been cooked on a barbecue. Shiraz can take even more spice.

Italian reds e.g. Barolo, top Tuscan reds like Chianti: Always best enjoyed with classic Italian food, preferably from the region. Barolo is particularly good with braised beef, game, rich pasta and truffles. Chianti shines with Italian-style roast lamb and veal and with baked pasta dishes like lasagne.

Rioja and other Spanish reds: With the revolution in Spanish winemaking, Spanish reds are changing faster than you can say paella. The typical style used to be exemplified by Rioja Reservas and Gran Reservas with their soft, delicate fruit and gentle tannins (good with grilled lamb, game, sheeps' cheeses and subtly spiced stews and tagines), but the new wave of reds can handle much more robust flavours – more like a Cabernet Sauvignon or top Tuscan red, as previously.

Zinfandel, Pinotage and other rustic reds: These are ideal for your heartiest meals like big rich meaty stews and braises. Also good with a cheeseboard.

Sweet wines: Top dessert wines like Sauternes are at their best with simple fruit tarts, especially apple, pear, peach or nectarine-based ones and strawberry tarts with crème pâtissière (cream helps to show off sweet wines). You can also drink them with foie gras or other rich liver pâtés and with blue cheese (the latter also being the classic way to enjoy vintage port).

Champagne: Champagne is a surprisingly flexible partner for food, particularly eggs and seafood and also handles Asian cuisines well, especially Chinese and Japanese food. A glass of sweet (demi-sec) Champagne is also a glamorous way to finish off a special meal – it goes well with gâteaux and other celebration cakes. *See Food and Fizz, page 113.*

frequently asked questions

WHAT SORT OF WINE GLASSES DO I NEED?

Ideally, it's useful to have four different types – a generously sized wine glass for red wines, a smaller one for white wines, a set of tall Champagne flutes and a set of small glasses for sherry, port and dessert wines.

HOW LONG DO I NEED TO CHILL WINE FOR?

It depends on the wine. Most people tend to serve white wines too cold and red wines too warm. Champagne and dessert wines need chilling longest (about 1½–2 hours, depending on the temperature of your fridge), crisp dry whites need about about 1–1½ hours, full-bodied whites and light reds about 45 minutes to an hour. Even full-bodied reds benefit from being served cool rather than at room temperature (about 15–18°C), so keep them in a cooler area before serving.

HOW MUCH WINE SHOULD YOU POUR IN A GLASS?

Don't fill it more than two-thirds full. Not out of meanness, but so that you can appreciate its aromas.

HOW LONG SHOULD I OPEN RED WINES BEFORE THE MEAL?

Its only worth opening them ahead if you're going to decant them. Otherwise not much air can get into the bottle. Most wines are designed to be drunk direct from the bottle these days.

WHEN SHOULD I DECANT A WINE?

Only when it's very full bodied and tannic or has thrown a deposit like vintage port. Be careful about decanting older reds. If they're very old and fragile, they may lose their delicate flavours when exposed to air.

HOW DO I DO IT?

Leave the bottle upright for at least 24 hours before you plan to serve it (so that any deposit can settle). Then, with a light behind the neck of the bottle, pour slowly and steadily into the decanter without stopping until you see the sediment inch towards the neck of the bottle.

HOW DO I TELL IF A WINE IS CORKED?

If it tastes musty or stale, there almost certainly is something wrong with it and you're perfectly within your rights to reject it (so long as you don't drink half the bottle first!). If it's simply too sweet or too sharp for your taste, then you've got no real grounds to send it back. The grey area is with older wines or ones made from less common grape varieties which may have funky flavours that aren't to your taste. But if a supplier or restaurant values your goodwill, they will replace it.

IF I'M INVITED TO DINNER SHOULD I TAKE A BOTTLE AND, IF SO, WHAT TYPE?

It depends how well you know your hosts. If you don't know them well, you don't want to imply that they won't serve you a decent bottle, so it's better to take something indulgent like a bottle of Champagne or a special dessert wine that could be construed as a gift. With good friends it's fine to ask what they'd like you to bring or what they're making so that you can choose something appropriate.

HOW MANY BOTTLES SHOULD YOU TAKE?

It depends on the numbers. For four of you one is fine, although if you're cautious by nature you could always take a back-up in case one is corked. For six or eight people you might want to take two (it's better to take the same type so that everyone gets a chance to try it).

SHOULD YOU OPEN THE WINE YOUR GUESTS HAVE BROUGHT?

The trickiest issue I find! It depends how it's presented. If they bring along an unchilled bottle of Champagne, I think it's fair to accept that it is intended as a private treat to enjoy on another occasion. If they produce a bottle that they're clearly excited about, the indications are that they want to share it with you.

useful websites

WINE AND SPIRITS

www.matchingfoodandwine.com
My own website with detailed recommendations on matching wine and other drinks with food.

Berry Bros & Rudd
www.bbr.com
0870 900 4300
Long-established London wine merchant with tremendous expertise and a wide-ranging list.

Adnams
www.adnamswines.co.uk
A big name in East Anglia (they brew beer and run pubs too). Particularly good for characterful mid-priced wines.

Lay & Wheeler
www.laywheeler.com
Colchester-based wine merchant, good for fine wines.

Tanners
www.tanners-wines.co.uk
Traditional country wine merchant with a strong range and good personal service.

GENERAL

Daylesford Organic
www.daylesfordorganic.com
A wide range of organic food from beautifully designed farm complex in Staffordshire and a new London shop in Pimlico.

www.foodfullstop.com
Effectively an on-line farmer's market supplying food from many of Britain's best producers.

Fortnum & Mason
www.fortnumandmason.com
Splendidly glitzy food hall. Strong on traditional British products including tea. Good wine department.

www.natoora.co.uk
Started off supplying French charcuterie and cheeses, now also sources from Italy and within the UK.

CHEESE

La Fromagerie
www.lafromagerie.co.uk
London's most fascinating cheese shop with branches in Marylebone and Highbury. Cheeses you can't find elsewhere.

The Fine Cheese Company
www.finecheese.co.uk
Excellent Bath-based cheese shop and mail order business. Ideal for gifts.

Neal's Yard Dairy
www.nealsyarddairy.co.uk
British and Irish cheeses, kept in perfect condition. Branches in London's Borough Market and Covent Garden.

MEAT

Brown Cow Organics
www.browncoworganics.co.uk
Award-winning West Country based meat and vegetable supplier. Particularly good beef.

Donald Russell
www.donaldrussell.com
Although this Scottish based firm has expanded into seafood it's known for its meat, especially steak.

Sheepdrove Organic
www.sheepdrove.com
Very well run on-line operation with well-butchered, well-packaged meat. Shops in Bristol and London.

FISH

The Fish Society
www.thefishsociety.co.uk
Supplies a wide range of freshly frozen fish including ready-made products like fishcakes.

Ummera
www.ummera.com
Top quality Irish Smoked salmon.

MARKETS AND FRESH PRODUCE

www.farmersmarkets.net
*The National Association of Farmers' Markets
Provides an up-to-date listing of farmers' markets throughout Britain.*

Riverford Organic Vegetables
www.riverford.co.uk
Based in Devon, now has one of the biggest vegetable box schemes in the UK.

The Herb Farm
www.theherbfarm.co.uk
Marvellous selection of live herb plants delivered to your door, including numerous varieties of oregano and rosemary.

BAKERS

Baker & Spice
www.bakerandspice.com
Fabulous baker and deli with 4 London branches with a limited but beautifully packaged range of mail order goods.

Paul
www.paul-uk.com
French bakery and pâtisserie with branches across London.

CHOCOLATE

Chocolate Trading Company
www.chocolatetradingco.com
The largest on-line chocolate shop in the UK, specializing in fine chocolates from around the world from cocoa to couverture.

Hotel Chocolat
www.hotelchocolat.co.uk
Real, authentic and exclusive chocolates by post and through Hotel Chocolat shops.

Rococo
www.rococochocolates.com
Beautifully presented and packaged chocolates, many of which have unusual flavours.

INTERNATIONAL FOODS

Brindisa
www.brindisa.com
All things Spanish, including beans and pulses, charcuterie, cheese, tinned fish, fruit, ham, honey, oils and vinegars, olives, rice and authentic paella pans.

Le Fruitier
www.lefruitier.com
Internet shop for the food of Provence. Ships worldwide. A wide selection including olives, tapenades, aubergine caviar, dried tomato caviar, olive oil, honey and jams.

Maroque
www.maroque.co.uk
Moroccan ingredients such as preserved lemons, mint tea, spices blends, tagine sauces and ready-made Moroccan appetizers.

Seasoned Pioneers
www.seasonedpioneers.co.uk
Excellent range of freshly ground spices and spice blends.

Valvona & Crolla
www.valvonacrolla.co.uk
Superb Edinburgh-based deli and wine merchant.

OTHER

Meg Rivers
www.megrivers.com
Traditionally baked British cakes, made in the Cotswolds.

Wendy Brandon
www.wendybrandon.co.uk
Delicious home-made jams and chutneys from Pembrokeshire in Wales.

index

acknowledgements

My grateful thanks to the friends who have shared the meals in this book, especially Richard and Tracey. My love, as always, to my husband Trevor, who uncomplainingly puts up with being experimented on and the ensuing chaos in the kitchen. For my children, Will, Jo, Kate and Flyn: here's hoping these recipes will stand you in good stead. And you, Maria, too. For my mother and mother-in-law – this is what I get up to! To all at my publishers, Ryland Peters and Small especially, Alison, Ann and Julia. Thanks for letting me do such a fun book. And to Steve, Peter, Annie and Helen – many thanks for making it all look so utterly gorgeous.

The publishers would like to say thank you to all our models: Helen Trent, Ros Campbell, Adam Wilkie, Zoe Lynch-Bell, Luke and especially baby Jake (Helen's godson). Thanks also to Anna at Maiden for the loan of beautiful homewares. For more information on Maiden's products and services visit www.maiden-uk.com.